BIOCHEMISTRY
FOR POETS
LIVING IN A CELL

HARI HYDE

ISBN (e-book): 979-8-9867181-7-0
ISBN (paperback): 979-8-9867181-8-7

Book cover design and editing by ebooklaunch.com

What is Life? A biochemist mischievously reimagines the lives of the cell's biomolecules. We fancy that we are reciprocally alive with the proteins, nucleic acids, carbohydrates, and lipids inhabiting our bodies. Yet we can sense that paramount insights—vital truths that the biomolecules warily guard from our scrutiny—still elude us.

Contents

PART I:

beasts in the bags

AUNTIE'S PET PROTEIN

"Loyalty, devotion, playfulness,"
said my aunt, describing the attributes
sought in her new pet. Her beloved dog,
Marley, died last month, gashing a gap
in her soul, so she said. Despite his warm
and affectionate nature, Marley exhibited
an untrainable attitude, sporadically obeying

commands, but disposed to race off whenever
directed to sit. One glance in his eyes confirmed
the innate intelligence behind his retinas. He
understood what action was proposed. He
smiled. His eyelids squeezed shut. He bolted as if
fleeing from a terrible truth. Often, he barked
at those episodes, redeeming his perspective.

My aunt hoped for a replacement pet inclined
to please his owner and display flexibility
to the indignations of socialization. Friends
suggested to her that she search her gut
microbiome for a tyke who would bond
faithfully and steadfastly to her, probably one
special Lactobacillus, unlikely to betray

her trust and cause appendicitis or sepsis.
This biddable little beast would deferentially
learn all his tricks and afford an inimitable match
for the unconditional love of his master. Moreover,
no sadness would darken his departure one day.
Divestiture, not death, on mutually agreeable terms,
imparts the impetus to slide from the groaning

GI tract. Even so, my aunt voiced her misgivings
about the brevity of her companionship
with a fly-by-night friend. Her nephew suggested
she consider adopting Titin, a monstrously big
protein found in her muscles, especially her heart.
The largest protein she owns, Titin functions
as a springy molecule, enabling muscles to contract

and relax without coming apart at the seams.
Auntie took Titin to heart forthwith. Indeed, Titin
had played with her heart all along. Besting
her departed dog in key attributes, Titin seemed
friendly and didn't get anxiety fits when left alone.
He never peed on our rug, and he calmed down fast
if spooked. He never barked more than his master

and remained affectionate, even when ignored.
Auntie and Titin loved to take walks in the park.
Titin adored Auntie's massages. She felt him
walking faster then. Titin loved new toys, new

experiences conveyed clandestinely by Auntie, who fancied she felt Titin's tail wagging when she fed him his and her favorite snacks.

After a while, Auntie began to miss Marley. When a neighbor's dog barked, she felt reminded of Marley's impetuous mischief. Her routines got disrupted by his impulsive spirit of inquiry. Marley reminded her that rules really don't matter. Best of all, when she vociferously yawned, Marley yawned too.

THE IMPERSONATION

Confidante, coach, consigliere,
enzyme, thymidylate synthase
engenders, provokes, catalyzes
the riot, the reaction, the transmogrification
of deoxyuridine monophosphate into
deoxythymidine monophosphate.

The passage proceeds with perfection,
thereby partitioning the signature ingredients
of RNA and DNA.

A gorgeous dimer of coils and five-stranded foil,
the TS enzyme snatches a handy tool in the cell,
5,10-methylenetetrahydrofolate, to actuate
the reductive methylation reaction. The active
site of the enzyme twists and pivots as key
protein side chains surgically implant the
methyl moiety that launches thymidine's later
capers in genes.

Alive for a few hours, TS recasts the identity
of its jolly prey into another distinct essence.
Thousands of molecules per second are
erased and created by TS. Each dUMP
and dTMP exists privately, as wholly defined

and demarcated as integers, a "1" and a "2."
Though TS wigwags and squirms, it snaps
back into shape when one cycle is discharged.

All players know their lines. TS divined all its
histrionics from birth, without one rehearsal.
Though the theater gathers a swarm of actors,
TS owns its role. No attempts will commence
to cast another protagonist. No creature in creation
can do what TS does, as well or as stylishly.

Proteins are alive. People are their puppets.
We know personages esteem specialists:
"Better to do one thing right, than a million
things wrong, in installments." Yet human
specialists prove incapable of achieving
perfection, not even one sliver of sublimity.

The virtuoso violinist, alas, "could have been
better." The marathon runner "should've
moved faster." The brilliant researcher
"should have foreseen the next step."
Feats by geniuses never match expectations.
Juggle twelve balls? We can envisage twelve
more. Furthermore, most folks are amateurs,
dabbling in pastimes, taking one step up
the ladder to the immaculate, then concocting
what roosts at the top. To christen a fellow

"a catalyst for change" insults the miracles
of our masters who reside in our cells. Enzymes
open doors. Men look through the windows.

No human could conceive the life of a protein, by
only attending one performance at a local playhouse,
never glimpsing the action backstage, nor deducing
their motives when they wander the stage wings.

Biomolecules play ball together unwittingly, often
appearing to partake in sports. But they do not
conspire, do not willfully collaborate. Each unique,
autonomous protein plays alone, the only pathway
that manifests perfection. The pitcher won't throw
a split-finger fastball to please the left fielder,
nor attempt a knuckleball to humor the shortstop.
The curveball is his pitch; it works every time,
next time too. The infield and outfield don't ever
exist in his trance.

In faith and philosophy, goodness only abides in
the flawless. "Alive" grants too grand a term
for the machinations of men. None can name
one task that Mankind has not flubbed, bungled,
and misjudged. Miscues, blunders, backfires,
and screwups chaperone each hour of our
misadventures, broadcasting our gaffes
to whatever sentinels may perceive us.

Thousands of tiny maestros, vivified prodigies,
were spooned into the bucket of our body,
though *we* never arose as alive, merely a barrel
for life, the fishbowl for the goldfish within.
Our modest role sets the boundaries for our
inner angels and hidden imps, confined to strut
upon finite frontiers of our fleshy opera house,
an auditorium bereft of requisite acoustics
to decipher the arias of the diminutive divas.

Ancient alchemists sought to transform common
metals into gold and conquer deathly diseases.
Unknown to them, a greater miracle already abided
within them, transforming mRNA into protein—
to me, as amazing as recasting a cloud
as a cow. If rumors hold true, it happens.
But it could only happen if each of these
perfectionist sprites, each self-obsessed
enzyme, each steadfast, implacable catalyst,
sought to fulfill only one discrete quest, again
and again, without a perusal of its cryptic milieu.

Enzymes might seem crowded in their narrow
cells, but in spirit, they resemble glittering
stars in the galaxy, as alone as any entity
circling the heavens, adrift in the eminence
of individuality. A man's void can solicit
and hoard these countless minstrels, but

never render their songs. Units of life,
the proteins saunter as biological artistes,
each singing one song in perpetual bloom.

A neighborhood resides in a cell, when viewed
by an outsider, but proteins harbor no concept
of community. Each enzyme senses its
sentience, propounding no opinions on
whether another abstract life force exists. It
presumes all other creatures are mimicking
its grace, with credible pantomimes
of its gestures.

Let Mankind aspire to do likewise.
Some say we have been impersonators
from the start, copying the behaviors
of the ancient, unseen mentors within
our inner outposts. What soldier or chef
or raconteur or mechanic or craftsman
hasn't unknowingly aped the style
of these paragons, the illuminati of life?

Only these miniature magnificoes live.
They're pristinely alive,
though we're not.
Not yet.

PROTEIN PAINTING

When the Proteins Arts Council met
to discuss a major initiative toward
beautifying the dreary cytoplasmic side
of the cell membrane and the frayed
mitochondrial surfaces, tempers flared
and viewpoints diverged.

But most polypeptides felt pressured
to make a hasty decision when nonunion
biomolecules, lipid-y, sugary, gene-y
intruders, crashed the Council Hall
with a list of ideas, unsought advice.

On the first ballot, the Council agreed
to commission a local portrait painter,
to select the most beautiful biomolecule
as the subject for portrayal upon her
gargantuan canvas.

With few dissenters, the Council chose protein
p53 to serve as the esteemed artist, someone
uniquely endowed in artistic taste, and a gal
grandly esteemed as "Guardian of the Genome."

Protein p53 sniffs out DNA damage and arrests
cell cycle progression to stop further damage.

As a transcription factor, p53 hobnobbed with genes, reputably an excellent masseuse, not above accepting tips for special favors. During apoptosis, p53 rubs elbows with the legions of lipids populating the mitochondrial membrane.

Since p53 frequents local tattoo parlors, no one acted surprised when she sported glycosylation on her derriere. Though she's putatively a friend to all, the Council knew of her nasty side, too, when single point mutations turned her into a cancer-causing fiend. Wanting to court favor with p53's better angels and forbid her worst devils, the Council unanimously agreed that p53 merited this honor.

Besides, the Council knew p53 was a born artist. Known to be a "DNA mimic protein," she impersonates DNA. p53 employs some of her negatively charged and hydrophobic side chains to fool unwary protein companions into binding p53 rather than DNA, thereby modulating recombination and helicase activity. In essence, p53 evinces the artistic vision and empathetic immersion essential for her important new assignment as the cell's portrait painter.

Protein p53 feigned interest in painting
membrane lipids, then inveigled them
with promises to include lipids as resins
in the many oil-based portraits she'd planned.
And p53 placated the carbohydrates in
the cell with promises that they were ideal
for a revolutionary new adhesive that she
intended to use in the paints. Pigments
proved plentiful from heme, melanin,
and carotenoids suffusing blood and skin.

Miss p53 felt compelled by local standards
of celebrity to initially sketch the torso of DNA.
But p53 got bored with drafting this luminary,
whose celebrity bulldozes any attempt at
a creative vision. Even so, p53 grew perversely
charmed by the twisted ladder motif of the
molecule, which, to her, connoted the revolving
path taken through life. Moreover, the flimsy
rungs on the staircase, mere hydrogen bonds,
would falter under the weight of a wanderer.
Unpredictable interspersions of G-C rungs
with weaker A-T rungs seem designed to lull
the climber to a crash. p53 also esteemed
the antiparallel rails. The two strands of the
double helix march in opposite directions,
denoting the infinity of space. p53 admired

the alternating major and minor grooves
on the serpent caused by the queer geometry.

The angles of attachment for the bases to
the sugars are different on opposite sides
of the helix. The big grooves bestow a landing
port for proteins. p53 pondered a sketch she
might paint that could afford an emblematic
portrayal of the breathtaking, bubbling
genetic ladder. But p53 was a traditionalist
artist, and DNA seemed too eccentric to
be chosen as the most beautiful molecule
in the cell.

As a classicist painter, p53 scrutinized
the foremost elements of art: line, shape,
form, space, value, color, and texture.
Particular proteins snagged her attention,
perhaps more for their transient proximity
than their genuine novelty. But for an instant,
each seemed the most beautiful in the cell.

p53 liked the curved lines in the EF-P protein,
which conveyed a feeling of movement
and emotion. EF-P is a translation factor,
at work in the ribosome. Its three beta-barrel
domains look like wings, quite similar to
a tRNA shape.

Next, p53 admired inositol monophosphatase, which rather resembled a butterfly, with throbbing surfaces threatening flight.

As well, p53 esteemed glutathione, a tripeptide whose tiny size augmented its vital role as a pivotal antioxidant. Its monomer to dimer transition rather reminded p53 of a minimalist DNA, in its seesawing form.

On a different scale, p53 favored the major vault protein, involved in transport activities, which assembles a vast number of identical chains into a big box. p53 lauded the gathering of self into a united society.

Hemoglobin and cytochromes earned high marks for color, but their prevalence diminishes dazzle.

The spiral structure of alpha helices and the accordion structure of beta sheets, though gorgeous in essence, pervade the visage and viscera of most proteins, stereotyping the tribe, and cloaking the uniqueness of every protein crusader.

As Miss p53 plied her brush, the swampy cytoplasm streaked the paints on her canvas, hindering her efforts to collar the crux of each

protein she portrayed in her fanciful vignettes.
Miss p53 squinted at the immersed morass
bathing her world and slapping her cheeks.

Focusing acutely inside the soupy broth,
she pinpointed the imps that rule us all.
Glittering in the cell chowder, the bent,
polar boomerang structure of H_2O whirled.
Oxygen hogs hydrogen's electrons, and these
partially charged players assemble hydrogen
bonds throughout a watery world. This perfect
solvent, too perfect at times, is a clannish,
little tyke who spends its lifetime denying it.

No mere fluid and pH mastermind, water reigns
as biochemistry's most important reactant.
Our biomolecules are patched up with O and H
atoms donated by water. Water can jump in
or out of macromolecules, making hydrolysis
and dehydration possible.

Miss p53 recalled that water allowed her own
hydrophobic core to condense and her
folding to flower. Favorable entropy accrues
when water releases its holds on a folding
protein. "I'd be an unstable mess if you
loved me too much," said p53.

Miss p53's paint brush battled the gliding
current of our world's most beautiful
molecule, the aura in our pond,
the wand work in our milieu.

MUSSEL ADHESIVE PROTEIN: CUDDLY HUGGER

Every interloper writes his own RSVP.
Whereas burglars carry crowbars,
torches, lockpicks, and master keys,
the squatter aspires to inhabit your home.
The drifter strives to haunt your household.

Wave-swept rocky shores are home to mussels,
tenaciously attaching themselves to underwater
surfaces, after secreting a dollop of glue. In a few
minutes, the mussel can cling to the rock,
despite the turbulent watery world that rages

to dislodge him in thunderous foam. The mussel's
molecular tool for adhesion oozes out and onto
a boulder. The key ingredient of the cryptic sauce—
a writhing, repetitive, serpentine protein—bonds
mollusk and stone evermore. Chemical oxidations

of the proteins' sinuous strings, devised and invoked
by the ingenious mussel, staple the humble physique
of the shellfish onto the majestic mound of the rock.
Mussel glue scoffs at the doctrines of the upper-crust
protein kingdom. Lordly cosmopolitan proteins squat

like balls of yarn in an aristocrat's basket,
each wrapped uniquely and elegantly

to feature the grace of their faces.
Mussel proteins persist as unwound yarn,
a randomly wriggling rope on the ground.

Down and dirty, these commoner cables slog
at work deemed beneath the hoity-toity hauteur.
In addition, a mussel's long laces shun water,
the indispensable partner of proteins in our cells.
A rebel, guerilla, anarchist, and gatecrasher,

this quixotic protein stays dry in the most watery
realm. Though fish ever fail at shoving water away,
oceans fail in their quest to dislodge the obstinate
meatball in a shell. Like a meandering seed
in the wind, a mussel is planted in unfertile soil

and then stands as a statue. Some say our own
cytoplasm sits caged in cellular prisons. What
wistful protein, within, does not wish for flight
to fairy seas afar, to sail in an illicit quest?
A stranger asleep in an interminable wake!

GFP, Luciferin, and Tyrosinase in Gray

Fancy a sailor hoisting a lantern
in his tiny boat adrift in the vast
darkness of our gaseous ocean.

Fireflies might appear to search
for something lost, maybe dropped
during flight. But, in fact, the light

annoys them. Scares them too.
They think searchlights are stalking
them, never conceptualizing a role

for themselves in igniting the light.
Molecular pranksters inside them
play with matches. Bioluminescence

arises from biochemical reactions,
inexhaustible sparkles that bounce
back and forth in their chemical kettle.

Specialized arsonists emerged from proteins
or amino acid components, transformed
to luciferin gunpowder and luciferase pistol.

Luminous jellyfish cannot fathom that they
glow in the dark. They assume illumination
descends from the moon. But a night-light

launches in the bowels of the barrel-shaped
green fluorescent protein, snug in the jelly,
fishing for fun and a romp in the spotlight.

GFP wrenches its skeleton, tying a knot
in its heart until it fluoresces when struck
by incoming blue light. Electrons get thrilled,

emitting their ecstasy as green light.
This light cycle spins onward, torching
the torsos of bioluminescent beasts.

When a protein discovers it excels
at a task, it revisits its victory, a trillion
times more. Proteins, unlike men, revel

in a singular achievement, fulfilled
phenomenally well. Molecules collar
their calling, then hammer the nails.

None know the emotions of proteins.
Some imagine their lives dreary.
Some picture insentient serfs in a factory.

Survey your own senses to unmask the truth.
Hear the muffled mayhem that traverses
the plasm. View the shimmering winks,

rippling like raindrops in a pond, as dynamic
twitches in protein skeletons feverishly kink
in the commotion, a melee you can smell,

befuddling the tongue, like a bite of mango.
Feel the foment of carnage and amalgamation.
An uncharted carnival convulses within us.

Tyrosinase, a dignified, dour, and decorous protein,
schemes to conceal the pandemonium herein.
This oxidase deploys tyrosine to assemble a mask

of black melanin, a labyrinthine polymer renowned
as the pigmentation in our skin. Screaming white
tissues now bask in the shade. Like a sea's secret

affairs, a cell's sagas lie hidden beneath layers
of confounding curtains. Each molecule struts
its singular dance on the unutterable stage.

A Night in New Orleans with L10A Protein

On Bourbon Street, New Orleans, that night,
the man staggered through dense crowds,
bouncing off streetlamps, ricocheting
from random collisions with tourists
on the neon splashed walkway.

Pirouetting, pivoting, wheeling around,
he swayed and rebounded from jostles
and jolts from a restaurant wall or sightseer.
Inebriated, befuddled, and under the influence
of the booze broadcasting the name of this street,

he stumbled toward the doorway of Vieux Carré
Oyster Bar. The bar bouncer shoved him
back in the street, wherein he swiveled, spun twice,
and toppled flat on his back. His eyes stared
at the night sky, the firmament's divine sanctum.

Inside his eye, within one particular cell,
an intoxicated protein, drunk with desire,
shirked her duty to assemble her sons.
L10A helped with assembling the ribosome,
enabling its work in mRNA translation,

manufacturing any protein variety,
including more of herself. Dozens

of disparate proteins inhabit the ribosome,
and this L10A renegade posited
that the mound could get by without her.

Leaving her post, she meandered
the unmarked avenues of syrupy plasm,
bumping into mitochondria, skidding
on Golgi, entangling herself in metabolic
cycles that twirled like fallen leaves

in a whirling wind. Her quest
finally ended when she arrived
at the nuclear membrane. Gazing
through the veil, she beheld, in the fog,
chromosomes swaddling the delicate

DNA threads, the coils of yarn. She witnessed
huge proteins enter through nuclear pores,
polymerases and histones, who, like her,
nurtured a diversity of nucleic acids,
the glorified toolkit for proteins like her.

But the biased gatekeeper would not grant
her access. All around her, she spied hormones
and vitamins slip through the fence, chaperoned
by nuclear receptors, laughing in piggyback rides
to the genome. L10A descried injustice.

So, this is life's lesson, she thought. Be really big,
or small and cute. Be a prodigal son, not the one
who serves humbly and homely. Be famously
lost to arise eminently found. Cytoplasmic winds
scattered tatters of lipids shaved from the wall.

A loop in her belt fluttered with the feathery noise
of disappointment. The wall smelled like lard.
Then she gazed up at the grand curtain, the outer
cell membrane. Maybe grand decisions are decreed
beyond the burdensome codes of this chamber.

L-ASPARAGINASE: JUGGLER IN BONDAGE

Some say a man's greatest folly unfolds
when he attempts to be good at everything,
thereby ensuring he will excel at nothing.
A jack-of-all-trades, master of none, impresses
only the everyday idler with undersized problems.
Virtuosos, only, garner a flock of onlookers.
Specialists solve formidable, singular problems.

Inside every cellular factory, each worker zips
through its duty. Each enacts only one major
assignment. No one tries a new task. Each
understands its good fortune to luxuriate
in its status as minimalist maestro, undisputed
guru of its craft. In the grand scheme, they work
as a team, but bliss blossoms from local renown.

L-asparaginase works 24/7 in an *E. coli* factory.
An enzymatic cadet in a metabolic militia,
"ASNase" doesn't undertake the most high-profile
catalysis in the realm. But the elegance of its
dance dazzles even the DNA disciples. Converting
asparagine to aspartate by releasing ammonia,
ASNase employs a catalytic nucleophile, threonine,

on its polypeptide chain to stab asparagine,
and presto, a new amino acid emerges,
wizardry like that of a magician's wand.
ASNase assembles its torso from four identical
subunits, and this molecular machine chugs
like a four-cylinder engine while resembling
a quartet of carnations. The cytoplasm spins

around this convulsive four-wheeler, humming
like the chorus in *Madame Butterfly*. Neighborhood
enzymes stop and gawk. Some are driven
to blaspheme or, more often, whisper, "Man,
that guy is *good!*" Life in *E. coli* sustained ASNase,
swimmingly, until meddlers from the outside
upended its tranquility with a writ of foreign

conscription into an outlandish alien army.
Researchers in the outlands discovered
that some blood cancers, acute lymphoblastic
leukemia, "ALL," in particular, lost their abilities
to synthesize asparagine, thereby becoming
dependent on importing this amino acid
from the bloodstream. They fancied

that adding ASNase to cancer cell cultures
would thwart this malignancy. It worked!
In a wink, ASNase was dragged from its happy
bacterial home and injected into cancer-stricken

ALL patients, some of whom benefitted from this groundbreaking therapy. When in its *E. coli* shack, peers had nicknamed ASNase, "the Juggler,"

in admiration for its dynamic choreography. But now this alien human theater overwhelmed its aplomb. Insulted by brutes in the bloodstream, assaulted by immunological thugs, ASNase felt lonely and lost. Blood rolled like a river, dragging each protein like a leaf in the wind, sometimes randomly snagged on an odd fencepost, fluttering, then flying again.

Drafted to serve in foreign wars, ASNase no longer felt special, nearly descending to a jack-of-all-trades.

ZYMOGENS: PROTHROMBIN AND OTHER HOTHEADS

A hothead prowls the labyrinthine subways
crisscrossing our flesh. His hair-trigger fury
could bring our blood to a boil, but corrective

measures by neighborhood watchdogs restrain,
never tame, his simmering malice and sizzling
antipathy. Concealed in his pants, a knife

flutters, and he's obsessed by the urge to slash
one particular protein. He no longer recalls why,
only that he's doing like his daddy did. Family

feuds fester in the bloodstream, the submerged
jungle that liquifies life. Call him prothrombin,
or "PT," if you're reckless or a friend of the family.

Call his prey fibrinogen, another blood protein,
which, when surgically cleaved into fibrin, assembles
a blood clot. PT's not the surgeon. Not yet. First,

PT's handcuffs get gashed by the pruning scalpel of
prothrombinase, when someone notices a blood vessel
got ripped. The local cops only unshackle PT when

cracks in the dams threaten to sweep the cozy,
warm-water swimmers to the airy Otherside. Nicked
and unbound, PT metamorphizes to thrombin, the cold

stalker who lacerates fibrinogen's pivotal linkage
that transforms it to fibrin, which curdles and clots
on the spot. It's a messy affair, though. You really

can't trust unfettered thrombin, to leave well
enough alone. Thrombin's happy to trigger blood
clots outside his assigned workstation. If one bite

tastes good, ten might taste a magnitude better.
Thrombin knows he won't suffer a heart attack
and doesn't even care if you do. You can't reason

with a butcher who's carving a tenderloin. Thrombin's
fury tends to consume him after a short rampage,
but players walk on a tightrope in our eerie arena.

PT is a zymogen, the name for proenzymes whose
impulsive urge for demolition precludes a presence
in polite society. Most zymogens spawn proteases,

the ruffians of the cell. Death-dealing caspases
and microbe-mangling complement proteins
conceal their intentions in straitjacketed garb.

PT was born in the liver, but pancreatic zymogens
skulk like Rottweilers chained in the basement,
only released when robbers ransack your house.

Thank trypsinogen and proelastase for congenial
digestion. Food takes a beating, not those fed.
As zymogens, they slumber in dormancy, gently

coached on anger management. Sometimes,
stress can provoke certain irascible zymogens,
via autocatalytic proteolysis, to self-activate.

Zymogens emerge as active enzymes, when losing
a piece of their hearts. Their heartstrings get
chopped. The tranquil side of their disposition

suffers a lobotomy, an excision unbuttoning
scruples. Tiny zymogens grant to us, by proxy,
a premier model of our society's conundrum.

Our emotions smolder, not blaze, manacled
by irresolution toward fulfilling our passions.
A comrade's affront can propel us to execute

impulsive acts. Our yarn partially unravels,
and we emerge, breaching the border,
raring to sever a marionette's strings.

PROTEINS A, G, L, M DECOYS

Why are we captivated by theater?
A society's most disreputable
profession allures huge audiences that no
earnest family gathering could match.

A thespian labors as a licensed liar,
posing as another, pretending to live
a life lent from a stranger, detaching
her own life from the stooge on the stage.

Maybe the monstrous deceptions
of the arena's players make our own
life's lesser lies seem inconsequential,
in contrast. A bank robber will never get

charged with double-parking. The actors
pardon our artifice. After attending a play,
we feel genuine, when weighed against them.
Our own workaday episodes seem uplifted,

whatever rationalization or premise
we invent to discharge the duties determined
by external coercion. Anyway, our chosen
ruffles, frills, tinsel, and spangles stay true.

Besides, the players embolden us
to believe we can fit our wits and
physiques into anyone's personage,
and, likely, any creature's witchcraft.

Nature's artists confirm this conclusion.

Staphylococcus aureus infections arise
when these bacteria breach the skin barrier
and plunge into the bloodstream, possibly
provoking sepsis or endocarditis.

Staph compiles a rogues' gallery of proteins
to torment the host. Pore-forming toxins punch
holes in combative neutrophils' membranes.
Adhesions adhere to host tissues. Coagulases
form a protective fibrin capsule. Then Staph's
biological mimicry foils the host's immune response.

"Protein A" resides in Staph's cell wall
as a molecule with a mission. The polypeptide
sports five similar three-helix domains that
make the protein look like a ring of replicas.

Each domain can bind tightly to antibodies,
from the immunoglobulin G tribes, in their Fc
heavy-chain segments, regions required
for opsonization and phagocytosis, thereby
thwarting defensive immune cells from

destroying the pathogenic bacteria. Protein A
also blocks the formation of IgG hexamers
needed for activation of the complement system,
designed to punch holes in bacteria. Protein A
can even cross-link surface IgM on B cells,
leading to overproduction of nonspecific
antibodies, harmless to Staph.

IgG got accustomed to grasping Fc receptors,
which decorate immune cells, with a gentleman's
handshake, a perfunctory pressing of flesh.
But then Protein A came along, mimicked the
contours of Fc receptors, and refined his handshake
into a viselike clench. Protein A binds IgG with
higher affinity than cellular receptors do. The
multi-domain structure of Protein A allows hugs
to also arise, such that the disassociation of the
complex dawdles drastically, assuring high avidity.

To IgG, Protein A purrs, "I love you more. Free your
fantasies." Likely, the IgG antibody, a soldier sworn
to capturing invaders, might not be fooled by the
rigid embrace of Protein A. Rather, the IgG conjures
a vision of an elsewhere, that idyllic somewhere
where the past hours' boundaries vanish and new
ventures await, a frontier past the fences. The
sureness of the beaten path won't win over
a majestic molecule imagining quests.

Nature sprawls replete with dream weavers.

Streptococcus pyogenes infections also employ toxins and immune evasion, possibly leading to rheumatic fever or toxic shock syndrome. This bacterium's "Protein G" also binds IgG, though through differing contacts. Protein G also flaunts repetitive domains—some for binding IgG–Fc, some for binding IgG–Fab, and some for binding human serum albumin, HSA, the most abundant protein in blood plasma. Microbes are versatile. Whereas Protein A is predominantly alpha-helix and employs mainly hydrophobic contacts with Fc, Protein G is a four-stranded beta sheet with one alpha-helix across it. Its Fc complexes use mainly charged and polar contacts. The HSA binding domains employ an antiparallel three-helix bundle. The bacterium hitchhikes on HSA, as a camouflaged bug.

Microbe theater is resourceful. The masks of tragedy and comedy, one crying, one laughing, in practice symbolize the extremities of the many gradations inside. And the bacterial imposters seem realer than routine, run-of-the-mill life.

Finegoldia magna bacterium causes infections of soft tissues and bones with the nefarious

assistance of "Protein L," which, unlike Proteins
A and G, clutches all antibody classes by their
kappa light chains. Protein L flaunts tandem
repeats of its seductive domains, the better
to hogtie and thwart the antibody defenders.

Mycoplasma genitalium is sexually transmitted
and might cause cervical or urethral inflammation.
This bacterium's "Protein M" employs a unique
structure, as the most potent antibody blocker
of all. It binds both light chain types, and its
extended C-terminal domain physically obstructs
any IgG from grasping its assigned antigen.

Though tiny, Mycoplasma's genome invented a big
ruse, assembling a decoy to evade immune
destruction. Protein M units are displayed
on the Mycoplasma surface. Human antibodies
may then coat that Protein M-bedecked surface
with their humanity, rendering the invader
seemingly human. Maybe more so.

In life's theater, your false portrayal, of you,
liberates me. I may now conceive that my own
image is coequally false.

MICROBIOME GANGLAND

My excuse? I'm mostly prokaryotic.

Most of my cells lack a nucleus
or membrane-bound organelles.
I'm mainly a bag of unicellular
bugs. My body employs 100 times
more bacterial genes than
mammalian genes. Since I can't
live without them, my microbiome
call themselves human. Among the
thirty-some trillions of eukaryotic cells,
I fancy only one special brain cell
is quintessentially me. Probably one
unique axon or even one wise
neurotransmitter.

About five pounds of me are bugs.
Bacteria and yeast grow fast,
but they're puny punks compared

to my fat nucleated cells. Just
to humiliate them, I show off
my ovum, my biggest cell.

It makes them feel as small
as they are, maybe fifty times
smaller lengthwise, though they

point to some guy's sperm cells
and claim size equivalency. Truth
be told, guys can act pretty small too.

I'll bet one of my white cells,
which only stay white in my blood,
could swallow ten thousand bugs.

The bugs fancy that we're partners,
claiming they nourish me and fix up
my immunity. Bugs always claim

that they're heroic, saving the day
behind the scenes, beyond the spotlight.
Well, I'm the breadwinner in our family.

Every gourmet meal they've enjoyed
was purchased by me. Some of the bugs
squat on my skin, like bums at a train station,

but most of them cruise through my guts,
hitching a ride in a runaway boxcar.
You'd never guess how much mischief

they create down there. I know they're
having fun. I can hear the swing band,
the percussion, and the slide trombone.

Have you noticed that every community
gets divided into two quarrelsome camps?
My microbiome and me are like the Democratic

and Republican Parties. You've likely already
decided which one is which, proving my point.
Even our brain gets zipped up between two

hemispheres, and each bucket needs to stay
filled up with conflict, or we'd wobble and topple.
You're always, freely or fatefully, somebody's foil.

The bug gang trudges along my colon like tourists
at the Paris catacombs, but they launch like rockets
to Mars. Then they play dead, drowned maybe,

or asleep, I guess. Not comatose, though.
I know they're still thinking, the obsessed,
abstracted way that bugs do. You might guess

that they're planning their next adventure.
But I worry they're reading my thoughts that
this is as good as it gets, this side of paradise.

GLYCOSYLATION BOUFFANT

The Greek sea god Proteus, a slippery fellow,
evaded commitments by changing shape.
Grasp a handful of ocean. Your grip grapples
with the elusive convictions of all things.

Like Proteus, proteins squirm to escape
their skeletons. They twist and twitch
in persistent pulses as though ecstasy
provokes them to evoke rhumbas.

They like to think spontaneity launched
them into improvisational dancing.
But the choreography came preplanned,
like it does always, for molecules and men.

Gaze east or west, we're forever somewhere
in between the ripples' crowns and creases.
Like the trunk of an octopus, we're meant
to mark the mundane middle of it all.

Why do humans still sprout hair? Vanity
fuels the engine of natural selection.
Survival of the fittest faker still chaperones
our fortune. Eyebrows raise a response.

A patch of hair incites fantasies
more than a carpet of fur could do.
Accordingly, many proteins blossom
with glycosylation, long chains

of sugars dangling from their torsos.
Strutting down the Golgi runway,
each protein fashions its own headdress.
Braids, ponytails, dreadlocks, mohawks,

ducktails, bobs, and buns. Rarely, a buzz cut
crowns a coiffure. Feeble excuses are made.
"I sought my bouffant for practical purposes
… *um* … for better structural stability,

"prolonged stamina, protection against
highwaymen. It's my theater ticket
for admittance to the best box seat
at the pageant. Friends wouldn't know

"me with a retrograde bald head. If I'm lost, hair
affords recognition by search parties, semaphores
among friends. They're tresses, not beards."
One cannot wear too many masks in a jungle.

THE INNER OUTPOST OF THE CELL

The sun stooped.
The burst of brightening light
betrayed her frightened eye,

wrenched open that instant,
alarmed by the sight of me.
Or so I thought, but the sun

looked deep into the inner
outpost of one cell
that dazzled her eye.

One cell among my trillions
enraptured the sun. What
wonders must cluck in this coop!

Maybe a stem cell or ovum,
where grand episodes launch,
or maybe the cell creating

the muscle fibers for goose bumps.
Or maybe the muscle cells
in my ear meant to dog-flop

and pinpoint the location
of sounds, though I can't raise
them anymore, like a pooch does.

The sun burned through
the chosen cell's membrane,
and I peeked inside,

really squinting my eyes
and cupping my ears
to get the whole scene.

The bowels of a cell
throb like a shop of toy tops.
The wind ruffled my eyebrows

as I gaped within. Mitochondria
smoldered like dirigibles in flames,
red as a bonfire ablaze in the night.

Sniffing the smolder, I blew through
the hole, but regrettably fanned
conflagrations throughout the arena.

Green ribosomes glowed sinisterly, snug
on their phantasmal membranes.
Link after link crackled, *clink* after *clack*,

as chains of proteins elongated, like
a dangling icicle, but faster than thought,
maybe a dozen links per second,

like coupling train cars, locomotive
to caboose, before sent afloat to wad up,
crumple, and collapse into beach balls,

professional meddlers, kindhearted
mischief makers, but pitiless gladiators
who stick to the agenda. I tossed

a beer can into a lysosome trash can
and still recall the grinding clatter
that announced my error. An eerie

habitat haunts the cell. I expected
the crowded jelly inside of this shop,
but cytoplasm can surprise you.

It's a fantastically noisy place,
if you stick your ear in the goop,
and every organelle rings its own bell

at a distinct pitch, so the whole arena
reverberates like a cathedral on Sunday,
and your skull's part of the xylophone

if you plunge it into the syrup. To me,
the ballroom smells like a bakery.
The aroma arrives thrillingly fresh,

and, around every corner, a new
molecule flaunts its bouquet. I guess
the Golgi apparatus sitting on the slimy

carpet smells best, with the sugar cookies
topping the new protein kids. Okay, I
did lick the frosting, but I don't let

intimacy affect my judgment. What grabs
you most about this place is the motion.
Constant wiggling makes them look blurred,

but it sure looks like half the folks
are led on leashes. I think they'd all
congeal in a glob if they stopped moving.

Proteins routinely endure collisions,
and they grapple their partner like
sumo wrestlers until something or

nothing happens. There's no romance
involved. Believe me! But as players
mount and flee the stage, the foremost

feature is absence. One senses
that something remains missing,
and its abundance underscores

its deficiency. While I swam the
cytoplasm, the UV sunbeam finally
fractured the nuclear membrane

and lanced the DNA, maybe
in a random base, a C or T, I think.
Two adjacent bases fused,

and I knew that kink in the zipper
would lead to a mutation. You know
what happens to your pants zipper

when that happens. You can't refit it
and have to hope the slider that engages
the teeth can plow through the snag.

It probably won't, and you need to fix it.
My fix-it guy in DNA repair never showed
up. Probably drunk. It's my cell, after all.

I don't think the sun planned to be mean.
She probably thought change is good.
You never know. I might get improved.

I don't think the sun is that *something*
that's missing in cells. But it's something
out there. Maybe something in the clouds

up there, like that wisp of rainbow
and that low laughing thunder. Here
comes the rain, so I need to shut up.

KREBS CYCLE ORCHESTRA

Free-floating, squishy blimps,
packed with arrays of bioelectronic units
that generate the cell's energy stores—
ATP, the constant coin of the realm—
meander the syrupy swampland.

These mitochondria sizzle like fraternity row
on a hard-partying college campus.
A carnival convulses, roils, foams, froths,
and romps. Unbeknownst to present-day probes,
mitochondria reverberate with music.

Cellular respiration transforms glucose to ATP
in three distinct dogmatical venues.
Hear the singing chefs crooning in cytoplasmic
patio kitchens and grill stations,
flipping spinning pizza dough high in the air.

That's glycolysis, the start of cellular dining.
The finale, oxidative phosphorylation, occurs
in the inner membrane of the mitochondria.
There, wee electricians work as a bucket brigade,
hurrying electrons to forsake their energy

along the cascading chain of proton pumps
until electrons meet oxygen, which splits

in half and snatches protons to form water.
This finale perpetually crackles and smolders.
You smell it if you're wearing damp socks.

But the thrilling stuff always happens in between
packing and unpacking your luggage on any
safari. The middlemost mayhem, the Krebs cycle,
foments in the murky mitochondrial matrix. There,
a merry-go-round of eight enzymes further digests

glycolysis's first fruits to produce energy, which gets
packaged in NADH and FADH2, two deputy electron
carriers who work with the bigwig, ATP, later on.
It's really a cycle, too, because the chain of events
regenerates oxaloacetate, the starting chewable

snack of the whole astonishing orbit. Unlike some
smart proteins, the eight enzyme revelers in the Krebs
gang don't really know what they're doing. Another
spin about the circle calls for another round at the pub.
They're unaware that their assembly line connects

to a purpose beyond their collegial shop. They live
for the moment, intoxicated by the buzz of chemical
transformation. They've flocked as a musical combo,
each with a nickname, a handle that serves
as an alias among chums. "City Sin" kicks off

every cycle with a sax solo that rattles the crystal
on the chandeliers when the acetyl garnish leaps
aboard their vittles. "Anaconda" joins in on clarinet,
wailing a maelstrom just as the hydroxyl group flips.
"Izzo de Hyde" tortures his trumpet until one carbon

dioxide flies the coop and NADH has snatched
its electron. "Key Glue," the band's trombonist,
arises from the shadows. He harbors a flair for
flamboyance, soaring to heights not yet reached
by his bandmates. As the slide slithers, electrons

glide. His horn howls, grumbles, and brawls.
Another carbon dioxide somersaults. One NADH
leaps. And somehow, no one quite knows how,
a coenzyme A links onto the end of the trimmed
molecule like an unctuous caboose.

That's when "Sushi-TK" raises his trumpet
as though hoisting binoculars to gaze into
another dimension. The trumpeter is known
for injecting tumultuous motion into his melodies,
painting a sound portrait of the wildland he

perceives. As the coenzyme A exits, a GTP
songbird springs out, spontaneously engaging
the horn player in an outlandish duet. Next,
the flutist, "Subtle Sate de Drogen," mellows
the mayhem just a bit, almost playing pianissimo

for most of this gig. You'd expect the two hydrogens
from the succinate molecule to flip explosively onto
an FAD coenzyme, but the transfer coasts so artfully
that you don't even notice a thing except the rigid
carbon double bond now in the middle of fumarate.

That double bond doesn't last long. "Fumes,"
the band's violinist, fights with his fiddle until
the mitochondrial membranes start peeling.
Water molecules jump for cover, and one
of them plunges into the midst of the fumarate,

adding a hydroxyl group and its new sobriquet,
malate. Then it's time for "Mallet" to pound
the skins. Mallet's the kettledrum virtuoso who
can surprisingly play a full musical scale on
his drum by striking varying spots on the skin.

In a wink, the new hydroxyl loses a hydrogen,
while yet another NADH erupts from the party.
The final product, oxaloacetate, is ready for
City Sin to start a new cycle. But first, the beer
guzzling troupe always plays the first four notes

of Beethoven's Fifth Symphony, commemorating
their successful voyage through the carousal.
Maybe a minute passes to complete a full round.
And on each cycle, their gallant groceries donate
electrons and energy to cellmates in greater need.

The Krebs cycle octet plays a different song
on each cycle's orbit, though the cuisine
and feast remain veritably the same every time.
Each splinter of time rolls past gloriously,
grandly the same, regally distinct, evermore.

Fancy how this musical combo perceives,
partakes, and sustains the ecstasy!
Imagine if all five of your senses were erased,
then restored, every second. The ravishing
newness remains radiant forever.

THE BEAST I MURDERED

If we'd chanced upon each other
in some pastoral precinct of the blood,
I'd likely have nudged him impishly
and swapped stories about the gridlock

at the emerging plaque in our host's
carotid artery. But at this hour, I glared
into his face and slashed him where
he perched, and he fell headlong, dead.

Call me NE, neutrophil elastase, the body's
lunatic, some say, a maniacal assassin
caged in N cell granules with the most
callous killers known to Mankind.

We, the brutal, are shunned by civil
society until our barbarity serves
to maintain the ennui of the comfortable.
Sprung from my cage, I rampaged.

The beast I murdered was a *Shigella* bacterium.
Ripping his outer membrane protein
to shreds, I startled myself with a tinge
of remorse, apropos my brutal deportment.

Enlisting in opposing armies, the Shig
and I, both unemployed, fancied to sign up
in clashing camps in the war. I never
deciphered what harm he intended,

to me personally, I mean. Yet I knew,
I *felt*, he was my foe. I suspect he schemed
to kill me through circuitous measures
by killing my friends, my family, though now

I question the friendship and filial affection
of any outcast or insider in or out of my cell.
My cutthroat capacity arose as a compulsion,

imposed externally, not sought or selected by me.
Rumors abound in this neighborhood of an *outdoors*,
so we call it, where savage dogs often kill dozens

of fowl and eat not a one. Killing's an instinct.
You eat only when hungry. Though never hungry,
I bite for the thrill. I twist, flex, contort, buckle,

and bend my skeleton until my active catalytic
site slits the throat of my prey. Then it's over.
I feel nothing except an impulse to do it again.

I'm a renegade now, slashing any tissue I meet.
I get blamed for COPD, pulmonary fibrosis,
cancer growth, metastasis, and liver disease.

Lawmen chase me, alpha-1 antitrypsin for one,
trying to keep me from doing what I do.
Somehow, that adds to the excitement,

the thought that I might get caught,
the thought that they might quell my innate
addiction, the thought that better fun exists.

RNA Contrarian

Thankful that she's assigned
the most thankless tasks,
RNA prefers to perform uncanny
feats in private. Contemptuous
of applause, she ducks praise,
not from false modesty. Rather,
she foresees any acclaim afforded
to her would be insultingly insufficient.

In a cellular world of bombastic
enzymes and prima donna DNA,
RNA cruises quietly crucial.

Her sardonic temperament arose
in reaction to the fatuous celebrities
who misuse their mainstage to misquote
biology. She plots the revival of an
RNA World.

RNA is a contrarian who presumes
any assertion made by a polymer
longer or fatter than her is wrong.

"Why is RNA transcription named thus?"
she'll inquire. "Though an RNA transcript
is the product, RNA does not undergo

transcription. Rather, DNA does, so name it,
DNA transcription.

"Transcription is the action or process of
transcribing something. Only the *something*
that already exists can experience transcription.
Also, why won't you therefore name the work
of reverse transcriptase, 'DNA transcription?'

"Audio transcription converts spoken words,
existing in an audio recording, into written text.
No one calls audio transcription 'text transcription.'
And no one should misname DNA transcription
as RNA transcription."

Sometimes RNA needs to get stuff off her chest,
and biomolecules grew accustomed to humoring
her rants. They know RNA is the roustabout,
odd-jobber, and Miss Fixit in their coliseum,
and no one ever rebuffs her tirades. The whole
factory gets shut down when she's on vacation,
which, fortunately, lasts only for a second or so.

From grunt work to scut work to dirty work,
she labors in the backscenes, far from the
floodlights.

A confirmed bachelorette, RNA relishes
her singlehood, sometimes reaching around

her lithe torso to base-pair with herself. She
never compromises her individuality, not
for long, but those hairpins she forms imbue
her with countless countenances.

A gal for all seasons, she's sometimes short,
sometimes long. As mRNA, tRNA, rRNA,
miRNA, siRNA, snRNA, she's courier, facilitator,
scaffold, signaler, and regulator. As the most
versatile molecule, she gets teased about not
perfecting one task. In RNA viruses, she's the
genome, at least for a while. Although
a credible enzyme, she can't compete
with protein catalysts.

She insisted on her distinct selfhood, marked
with uracil bases and ribosyl sugars. Getting
her longest strings spliced—nipped and retied—
was her idea initially, too, but then the enzymes
made a game of it, and it got out of hand. Now,
it seems nearly every mRNA sequence undergoes
alternative splicing, encoding distinct proteins
from the original scroll.

The microRNAs were her idea, a way to bind to
mRNAs and destroy them—gene expression
regulation on a grand scale. She's especially
proud of a special RNA, Xist, that targets one

copy of the two X chromosomes, inactivating
its redundant gene expression with a bit
of help from other braggadocio biomolecules.
LINE-1 reverse transcriptase sometimes
converts her to DNA for adventures in
retrotransposon insertions in the genome,
a risky game eschewed by sensible RNAs.

A couple hundred, various, biochemical
modifications festoon RNAs inside the cells,
selected by her to further customize each
family member. Her goal is to make
every child unique. And in private riot.

BELLY FAT

You gotta love a fat guy.
I'm thinking of those guys
who stay fat willingly and
by preference. See that guy
at the bar with a beer belly
the size of a watermelon?
He's judicious. He's rational.
Food is savory and abundant.
In brief life, eat heaps of it.

A buffet spreads as entities
once alive, now deceased.
Resurrect the dead for new
life in your flesh. Fat guys
always look twice as alive.
Passion gurgles and squirts
from the obese. You feel
they own a larger niche in
the world. You feel the weight
of their defiance. "Take a
good look. I've swallowed
your parcel. I wear it with
swagger."

But stare deeply into the mound
of fat drooping over his belt. Gaze
under the skin to view the hundred
billion fat cells, adipocytes, storing
lipids as energy munitions. Adipose
tissue sustains loose connections,
fostering the jiggles of the belly.

Within adipocytes, two tribes of lipids
claim their own space and frequently
feud about philosophical matters.

Triglycerides lounge around in the
cytoplasm as chubby spherical lipid
droplets. None display any eagerness
to do anything at all, though they think
deep thoughts.

Triglycerides are packed like sardines.
In the unlikely event of this fat chap
beginning a diet, hormones will
summon their disassembly to glycerol
and fatty acids as fuel for the furnace.
They'll insist on limousine service, however,
hitchhiking a ride on albumin or some other
blood protein.

The other tribe, found in the plasma membrane,
assembles a phospholipid bilayer surrounding

the entire adipocyte cell. This milieu is as greasy
as the triglyceride droplets, but, in contrast,
the membrane flows as a fluidic mosaic with
the imbedded lipids evincing more pep than
a puppy. They're always busy and loving it.

Hence, these tribes battle in metaphysical
disputes, pondering existence, possibility
and necessity, space and time, and, especially,
the abstract worth of motives and movement.

Structure determines function, and some
would say that their designs divulge their
kindred yet contrary destinies.

No mysteries persist about why triglycerides
are such a greasy lot. Their key components,
fatty acids, are long hydrocarbon chains, evocative
of organic chemicals who have not yet championed
the inclusion of oxygen and nitrogen atoms that
afford a plethora of bonding arrangements used
by biomolecules. The string of linked carbons
zigzag, sporting only bulging hydrogen atoms,
but a terminal carboxyl group permits attachment
to each of glycerol's three hydroxyls.

In phospholipids, only two fatty acids are linked
to glycerol. The final linkage attaches a phosphate
moiety, a charged group that bobs up on the outer

aqueous sides of the membrane. Hence, the buried,
inner lipid layer features two streams of hydrocarbon
tails swimming inside a membrane pond, back-to-back,
and side to side. Toss in a few cholesterol molecules
to spice up the stew.

Triglycerides and phospholipids both employ
a glycerol backbone. Some fatty acid components
are common to both tribes—palmitic acid, stearic
acid, oleic acid, and others. Both tribes use
saturated and unsaturated fatty acids. The
unsaturated carbon chains include at least one
double bond that improves fluidity. If not for
the various phosphate moieties in phospholipids,
the two tribes might reach a consensus.

Instead, quarrels sometimes get contentious.
The bloated triglyceride droplets sporadically
harass the plasma membrane, snatching lipids
to expand their dormant domain.

Phospholipids in the cell membrane
enjoy an exciting life, beyond affording
structural support for the cell. Membrane
lipids are guardians of the selectively
permeable barrier, the border wall
keeping invaders out, keeping citizens in.

They support active transport of new
immigrants, via channels and carrier
proteins. They house membrane protein
receptors that bind to hormones and
other signaling molecules in response
to external stimuli. They anchor cell
surface glycoproteins that permit cell
identification and communication.
They assemble the wire by which nerve
impulses travel. Life doesn't get
more exciting than that, so it seems.

But triglyceride droplets in the adipocyte
cytoplasm relish a calm, quiescent, abstract,
intuitive passion for each twinkling instant and
the glinting hereafter.

Phospholipids ask, "What will I make happen?"
Triglycerides ask, "What will happen to me?"
Remarkably, all joint attempts at formulation
of a unification theory have met with resistance,
even among the slipperiest lipids.

RIBOSOME MAGICIAN

We all know reality isn't.

Actuality persists unknown
to anyone.

Confronted with mysteries,
we believe an underlying
explanation prevails,
just out of reach.

Our foraging unearths
clarifications that merely
deepen the conundrum,
as metaphysical matters
arise.

Prior to international fame,
ribosomal RNA 28S worked
the carnival circuit as a magician,
performing remarkable feats,
which some say were illusions,
sleight of hand, misdirection,
perceptional manipulations, all
with reliance on duplicity,
though rRNA 28S insisted all
events were even more magical
than they appeared.

Sawing in half a lovely woman
who lay in a coffin, rRNA 28S
pulled the bisected box apart,
with the woman's head in one
half and her feet in the other half.
Detractors claim two different
women lay curled up in the two
halves of the coffin. The second woman
squirms to a hidden compartment
when the first woman is reassembled.

When rRNA 28S walked atop the water
in a swimming pool, skeptics claimed
that a plexiglass platform was concealed
just under the surface of the water.

Bored with these scoffers, rRNA 28S
decided to try his hand in the biomolecular
realm. This time, he focused on performing
one trick extremely well, rather than
endeavoring for versatility, and he chose
the most impossible feat ever conceived.
He aimed to transform a long string of
RNA into a long string of polypeptide,
which he called a protein. Blessed with
innate talents as a catalyst, he mastered,
uncannily, the peptide bond linkages
of amino acids into proteins.

His fame blossomed, and soon,
he enlisted a rapturous congregation
of molecules who were devoted to
fulfilling his dream. After innumerable
dress rehearsals, and with many new
members created by their clever
carpentry, a complete ribosome arose.

Eighty proteins joined his parish, and
three other rRNAs signed up too.
The final assembly was a beautiful mess,
with RNAs in helices, loops, and bubbles,
all wrapped around the eighty proteins
in the ribosome, which resembled swirled
chocolate syrup marbled into vanilla ice cream.
Two scoops perched atop the invisible cone.
Hydrogen bonds, electrostatic interactions,
and nonpolar contacts stabilize this
marvelous molecular machine.

At the peptidyl transferase center,
28S binds to incoming aminoacyl-tRNA
and the nascent peptide chain. There
he catalyzes peptide bond formation
between the amino acid ferried by the tRNA
and the growing protein cavalcade. Though
this synthesis relies on all the players
in the ribosome, 28S gets all the credit,

and everyone else presumes their roles
are merely to cheer his stunning successes.

Indeed, no one really believes this magic
is happening. A chain of messenger RNA
floats into their shop. A train of protein
floats out of their shop. The other members
of the ribosome chant hymns, sometimes
in unison.

At first, most cellular citizens thought
the chants arose to glorify 28S, who
got nicknamed "mustard seed," because
his tiny physique wrought such gargantuan
triumphs. But soon, matters were illumed:
28S performed the impossible. Ribosome
congregants prayed that no illusion
was perpetrated. If the impossible
proves possible, maybe someday
they might even glimpse actuality.

SKELETON DIEHARD

We'd been lying in this cave
for centuries before you found us.
Since you seemed surprised,
even delighted, by your discovery,
I presumed at first you spotted me,
proteoglycan 485739114, lounging
atop my former mansion of calcium
phosphate.

"Bones!" so you shrieked. I grasped
at once your bedazzlement at my
crumbling castle. Big things impress
big visitors. Candidly, I find the old
shop a letdown. I'd not known it
was even there, around me, until
the place began getting quiet and I'd
received no further assignments. Many
years passed until I could view the old
factory, and I couldn't quite piece it
together in my imagination. Lots of
long brown cylinders and one big sphere
with holes on one side. Maybe there's
something magical about the holes.

Though tiny by contrast, proteoglycans
are huge by protein standards. Our jobsite
is in the extracellular matrix, working
on the cell surface patrols. On my core
protein torso, I flaunt a few glycosaminoglycan
chains, linear polysaccharides. They somewhat
resemble a comb to outsiders, but the teeth
are built from chondroitin sulfate.

Back in the day, I worked hard at supporting
cell signaling, adhesion, and migration. Binding
growth factors always felt fun, but my steady
job entailed maintenance of structural integrity
of the neighborhood, by keeping the joint well
hydrated, and by tuning swelling pressure
in the milieu around the cells.

Nowadays, you'd barely recognize me.
I've gone to pieces, but never felt better.
My protein chain fragmented. Where there
was once a folded rope of beta sheet fabrics,
now find dozens of strands, none knowing
how the jigsaw reassembles after hydrolysis
splintered my cord. Most of my glutamine
and asparagine residues lost their amide caps.
My methionines are a mess, mostly oxidized
on the sulfur. My prolines are hydroxylated.
My arginines suffer citrullination. I see weird

phosphorylation on my hydroxyl residues,
and worse. Some advanced glycation
end-products tarnish my lysines and arginines,
thanks to the chemical Maillard reaction,
when sugars reacted with the free amines.
I'm mostly 2D now, having departed the 3D
world years ago.

The carbohydrate parts of me look just as
weathered. Microbes seem to enjoy feasting
on my sugary parts. Dr. Maillard messed
around with my polysaccharides, too, and it
looks like some parts of me got haphazardly
reassembled in a crazy quilt patchwork.

Truthfully, most of me disappeared entirely,
though I'm not sure where. But it's an exciting
leap into the ether. The biggest thrill is the
opportunity to be groceries for Nature. I'm
pretty much everywhere now, I guess.
Your front lawn and your Labrador retriever
are part proteoglycan 485739114, by now,
and part of you, too, I'll wager.

Maybe my whole time at work was a dry run
before beginning my real mission to colonize
the planet with me, one atom at a time.

I feel like my time living in the cell wrote
a story about me. Now Nature tore up my
manuscript, and, after all the edits, Her new
book tells a tale that's a tenth sequel of the
prior animation I endured.

Nobody I know comprehends this death
thing, which the outsiders are always talking
about. Maybe that describes the big slowdown
when I was furloughed. It was real strange,
but what isn't? Most of us referred to it as
work-life balance. You work passionately,
deliriously for a long while, then you drift
into life. The good stuff happens at the end.
You could never conceive just how good.

I've stared at my old mansion, that broken,
brown skeleton. I wonder if this thing ever
could conceptualize death. Look at the hole
in that big, empty skull. Whatever imagined
death is gone. Ever notice how these
ancient skulls all seem to be smiling?

PART II:

consciousness and outré outposts

THE HEART'S COLD CLOCK

Myosin, the molecule of motion,
appears grouchy during her duties
in skeletal muscle, like a caged beast
endeavoring to bolt.

But in heart muscle, myosin
cradles her passion. Hand over hand,
she pulls onward her actin partner,
much like pulling up a submerged
boat anchor, expecting her valentine
to surface at the end of the rope.

The heart chamber chorus chants,
"Suds-tub … suds-tub …"
Myosin savors the electricity,
relishes the climb. The filaments
slide. The muscle strikingly shortens.
Myosin finds no valentine waiting,
and actin filaments slide back down
to the seafloor. But myosin fosters faith.
On the next contraction, her paramour
will greet her at the end of the line.
"Suds-tub … suds-tub …"

Outside my window, the snowfall flows,
as if Time were finally announcing Itself,
as a visible, anatomical creature.

Pirouettes promenade, a little sloppy,
like a high school marching band
parading lackadaisically down Main Street.

The lawn remains green as ever because
the snowflakes climb up to descend
again and again in perpetuity.

Maybe they will never touch the ground,
though I sit here, stuck in gravity's
graveyard. My cold clock drums

somewhere inside me, somewhere
I've never seen. Time throbs there,
rapping the rhythm of humdrum wonder.

My heart's belts, chains, and gears
swivel and swing when runaway salts
soar through cell membranes.

I ate sodium and calcium last night.
Now they're electrified. But my heart
plods like a mechanical kitchen appliance,

rendering Time as a regimen. I fancy
the glorified heart myosin escaped
from prior assignments in the GI tract.

Outside me, the flowing white curtain
of Time awaits my crossing through
heavenly gates, when my cardiac

metronome collides with its coda.
I seem to arise as the snowflakes
halt, suspended in space. One

feels sure of unseen destinations,
thrumming, throbbing, drumming,
awaiting the stopping, awaiting the start.

DUMPSTER FROZEN DINNER IN MITOCHONDRIA

Outside my window, a bum hauled out
a paper plate topped with red spaghetti
from a snowy dumpster. Maybe he spied me
watching him and felt our eye contact
sanctioned his knock on my door.

He sought to use my microwave
to unthaw the frozen pasta.
I lied when I said that I don't own
a microwave oven, though my warm
wishes urged him to enjoy his meal

elsewhere. I don't want my oven
grungy and grubby from a stranger's
hasty and reckless misuse. Besides,
his request seemed impudent. Heat,
in private morsels, embodies our treasure.

A thousand tiny fireplaces, mitochondria,
dwell in most of our cells, churning out
chemical energy snacks, but also
spawning heat in our bodies as a byproduct.
These petite furnaces, however, are fragile.

Mutations, toxins, oxidants, and salt imbalances
wrench and rip them till the flames extinguish.

Eat right, try fasting, exercise more, but the bags
of chemo-electrical fire smolder and snuff
in the end. Mega-trillions of candles in my castle

expired already in age-ravished asphyxiation.
One by one, never two at a time, each puffing,
popping as bubbles, effervescing and sparkling
in the lifeless lather, a final time. Each campfire
flung a glowing grain off to the galaxies.

I've always hoarded heat, my earthly fortune.
But that bum's visit nettles me to this day.
I'd felt a strange warmth in his presence,
quite as though a communal heat
might smolder when two are gathered.

I've watched the dumpster every day,
half expecting his return, wondering
whether I might change my mind if he
beseeched me to thaw his daily bread.
Call it my further chance, not my final chance.

Two Proteins in an Old Soldiers' Home

"I've been battered, but I've kept my virtue,"
so said a protein to his comrade in an Old
Soldiers' Home for geriatric polypeptides.

Old friends from the dayshift in the nucleus,
histone H2AX and histone deacetylase SIRT1
served for months, so it seemed to them,

in maintaining genome stability and facilitating
DNA repair. Evading the proteasome dumpster
somehow, they settled in a fleeting sanctuary

for protein folk too damaged to serve any longer.
Protein turnover ravishes their ranks. Some chaps
last an hour or so. Those damaged get destroyed

so they don't make costly mistakes and harm
the health of the cellular community. Newly
synthesized copies of each protein, identical twins,

replace the decrepit oldsters. No special dumpster
exists to murder DNA, but when orders from above
tag DNA repair proteins with kiss-of-death ubiquitin,

the proteins get chopped, and so does the DNA
highway. Collagen, elastin, and, of course, dentin
are local legends, living forever, as far as we know.

For most proteins, long life means damage,
which means risks that the neighborhood
will deteriorate into a slum. Oxidation wrecks

proteins the most, though reactive oxygen
species ravage DNA and RNA, causing
8-oxoguanine scars and worse. Protein

amino acid side chains in methionine,
cysteine, lysine, arginine, and others,
when oxidized, tend to misfold.

Floppy, sloppy proteins make mistakes
on the job. Some even aggregate as globs
of useless refuse, prone to gum up the pulleys

and gears of cellular machines. H2AX and SIRT1,
timeworn, wistful, rocking gently in an Old Soldiers'
Home, swapped stories of the factory life.

"Amigo," said H2AX, "you've gathered a few more
nicks in your chain than I've seen in my days.
Yet my polymer's pendants suffered more scars

"than a whale in a shark tank. Take a look
at this methionine sulfoxide scar I acquired
in a fight with the O. This nitrated tyrosine

"still stings when I move. See this carbamylated
lysine? Got that one by sticking my neck out
to save the chromosome's skin. Really screwed

"up my normal protein handshakes. I've gotten
so flabby, I'm worried about aggregation
with friend or foe, the same. I suppose I'm

"a goner, for sure. But my compressed life
blazed in a lightning storm. Now lame,
now maimed, I surrendered myself to gain

"an invisible wisdom, a transcendent truth
that only failure unveils. I don't fear my own death;
I fear yours. For then death leapfrogs abstraction."

PRIONS AND PSEUDO-PRIONS

PrPC, the cellular prion protein, stroked
his sugary beard while curled in the gutter
of a slimy and slick neuron membrane.
Listless and seemingly inebriated, PrPC
evinced the mien of degeneracy, a skid row
bum spurning the civic duties of eager
beavers in the monotonous workaday world.

Awaking from his drunken bender, PrPC,
in a Kafkaesque epiphany, discerned
that his torso had warped into alien ribbons.
"Oooh boy, I really wrecked myself,
this time!" PrPC lamented. His familiar
alpha-helix skeleton, spirally spun, tightly coiled,
with every hand waving free in the streams,

had flopped out like a map of the world, which
proves impossible to refold right, and his frame
now resembled an accordion's furrows, layers
of flat beta-pleated sheet where his hands
grasped at each other between alternate rumples.
"Once a corkscrew of sorts, I seem to have
popped too many cabernets. Now I evoke

"a layered red velvet cake." Teased by peers
in prion society, PrPC endured taunts. "Call
him PrPSc," so they said, "scrapie prion protein,
a scourge, purveyor of neurodegenerative illness,
TSE, CJD, BSE, and chronic wasting diseases,
ravaging Mankind and beasts." PrPSc now forsook
his duties in cellular communications, which

seemed ill-defined in the first place, and just
lounged around the membrane, watching
the river flow and the groceries get delivered.
By and by, fellow PrPC dock workers began
to feel envy toward PrPSc's lethargic bliss,
and they took their lunch breaks on the same
park bench as their black sheep brother.

Soon pats on the back led to hugs and caresses,
maybe more, and everyone in the breakroom
began to metamorphose into beta sheet deformity.
The whole crew grew into slovenly laggards
that congregated in the smoking lounge, aggregating
as a blight on the sacrosanct cell. None of them
cared which disease they created, because all

the PrPSc knew they'd be dead before the big guy
around them finally faded to finale's finality.
"One bad apple spoils the bunch," so said
the PrPSc crew, laughing a little with the wistful,

bittersweet drollery for which prions are famous.
Indeed, transmissible prions, like airborne viruses,
never pin the blame on any one scoundrel.

In context of the big leagues, brain biochemistry,
amyloid-beta accumulation might initiate Alzheimer's
disease. "Aβ" parks in a nebulous status, named
a pseudo-prion. Though it misfolds and propagates
its deformity to neighboring Aβ, it's not highly
infectious, can't transmit disease, maybe merely
a bystander, unlike the highly infectious PrPSc.

Aβ never sought notoriety, unlike some rascals
we know in this pond. Of a philosophical bent,
Aβ adjudges life's big picture by enlarging its frame.
"Close your fist to point your random coiled finger
at me and, so you see, you're pointing three looped
turns of your protein chain right back at yourself."
A causation? Or a correlation? We've all been there.

SKATERS AND MYELIN

Avoid bruises. Master skating in youth.
Indeed, the enduring glow of skating
lingers in our memories of schooldays.
The blithe gliding feels emblematic
of freewheeling childhood. Old skaters
regret they started too late or too soon.
Elders can't be deceived by the euphoric,

laissez-faire illusion of flouting physics.
Then imagine the luxurious leisure
in the life of a membrane protein. Born
to float in a lipid bilayer, envied by every
pedestrian cellmate, these bobbers
often drift with the current, somersaulting
within the greasy river of jiggly fat.

They feel like they're floating in the Dead Sea,
with their bellies breaking the surface, much like
oceanic icebergs that park one piece in the air.
They feel like they're tubing down a gentle
stream, except water gets wilder, and lipids
bestow a feeble lift, like a bathtub of jelly.
Membrane proteins on the cell's exterior

rarely float around bald-headed. Party hats
of oligosaccharide chains festoon their pates.
It's so much fun that every molecule around
wants to take a dip in the wallow. But much
like skiers who desire a more challenging slope,
proteins discovered the axolemma membrane
around axons offers the ultimate titillation.

An axon serves as a nerve's electrical cable,
and the three-layered, bi-lipid axolemma cradles
ion channels spurting action potentials, voltage
spikes that send messages along frenzied nerves.
You tingle as you mingle in the blubbery flow.
Known as the paragon of pleasure, the Rafter's
Riviera, by vacationing peptides, the axolemma

flourished as the trendiest resort until protein
tourists discovered Myelin, that big canopy
overhead, which afforded an even grander holiday
haven. Myelin wraps insulation around the axon,
a fatty pillow that quickens nerve impulse conduction.
Myelin amasses cholesterol and saturated, long-chain
fatty acids, bolstering its stability. As luxurious

as butter, with warm ice rinks and fluffy ski slopes
in abundance, Myelin attracted year-round settlers,
MBP, PLP, and MPZ, for instance. MOG protein loved
the place and built a mansion on a hillside. MOG's

imperious demeanor rankled the local militias,
leading to autoimmune disorders like MOGAD,
maybe even abetting multiple sclerosis, which more

likely gets started by the inflammation instigated
by the roughnecks and hooligan tourists torturing
the skating arenas and ski lodges, tearing deep
tracks in the soft soapy hilltops. Over time, Myelin
crumbled and vanished, leaving the naked nerve
sputtering its faltering signals.

The elderly skaters retired to reminisce
on youth's gratuitous horizons.
And regret they started too late or too soon.

APOPTOSIS-INDUCING FACTOR (AIF)

Serenely safe, Queen Jeans reclined
on custom histone cushions, tugging
a shawl of attending enzymes around
her lithe torso. A baby maker, Jeans
purred when her slithering, serpentine
envoys launched as bookish ambassadors
through the drawbridge of her nuclear
castle, toting the edicts for the hoi polloi
cytoplasm, collectively craving her counsel.

Outsiders imagine a hushed Stygian dungeon
when envisioning the biological cell. They fancy,
incorrectly, that organ-type senses won't flourish
in these tiny precincts, these circumscribed,
quivering spheroids bagged by a bilayer
membrane. Indeed, the nucleus prefers to hide
beneath two sheets of phospholipid-laced quilts.

Extant, abiding, but beyond our cognition—though
wholly pervading our conception and awakening
our apprehension—biomolecules comprehend
each event in their shop and get addled, unhinged,
bewildered when, in captivity, they are enticed
to perform tricks in the test tube. Magnificent
stallions must feel this way when coaxed to count

numbers by tapping their hooves. Grandeur hibernates, hidden.

Radio waves brighten the hallways, perceived by all players. Though shadowy patches persist deep in the flesh, vain proteins may be noted combing their sugary coiffures, apprising their reflections on membranous mirrors. Sound waves thunder through bones. The submerged factory gets noisy if workers chat beyond whispers. Biomolecules smell trouble and sniff opened groceries. They're swimmers but don't call them fish. They collide with neighbors a billion times every second but might cross, like a careening drunk on Broadway Street, to the opposite side of the cell just as quickly. Consummately social by force, they bounce back to claim stoical selfhood. They can't hide their emotions. Silhouettes tremble like food blenders, but their passions play quietly.

Queen Jeans watched from the window of her nuclear citadel as the night shift workers executed her orders. Macabre mists crawled across the ER and Golgi, invoking on omen, a soothsayer's warning. Filaments twinkled as ATP gunpowder sparked. These railways rumbled eerily this eve, as though carrying coffins, as if each railcar ferried her foul, foreordained doom. Some sinister force stroked her double helical visage; perhaps the nuclear osmotic pressure suddenly surged.

Though music eternally sweeps through the cell, on
this night, dissonant chords infested ambient noise.
No cytochrome trilled. No coenzyme piped. No flavin
crooned. An alien sound, like squished tomatoes
or pumpkins flattened by a mallet, spurt through
corridors. Queen Jeans beheld a kingdom in chaos.

All forty-six appendages of Queen Jeans gaped
at the carnage befalling her tribe. Each denizen
was birthed or adopted by her. No one knew who
instigated the mitochondrial pathway of apoptosis.
Maybe some awful cellular stress or some tardy
growth factor had set mayhem in motion. She balked
at suggestions her damaged DNA spawned traitors
and cutthroats. Witnessing deaths in the factory
made death real. She couldn't conceive of an end
to her mission until her city teetered and toppled.
Cytochrome c bled from the mitochondrial rips. Its
red river conspired with APAF-1 to activate caspase-9,
then 3 and 7, executioner proteases that ravaged
her village. Innocent enzymes like PARP1 repairmen
fell early. No structural or signaling protein was safe.

Queen Jeans watched in a trance as her assassin
slithered from the mitochondrial cracks. A legend,
a specter, the wretched wraith resembled a floppy
pyramid, a pitiless hunter of the nucleic jewels.
Fiercer than caged apes, the thing acquired the

byname, "AIF," plying assonance to soften its
ghastliness. AIF savored the slow seconds needed
to translocate through the nuclear veil and
clutch Queen Jeans in a fatal embrace. Each twitch,
spasm, and lurch in AIF's grim advance toward
her throne queerly mollified Jeans. AIF's ever
pending proximity kindled her conviction that this
event happened only in some Otherworld to some
Otherqueen. When she felt the warmth of AIF's
snorts that brushed on her shawl, she demurred
to the candor and imminence of impossibility.

AIF wrought chromosomal condensation. Jeans's
robes fluttered to the floor in a hideous heap.
AIF freelanced as the foreman of apoptosis.
AIF never got blood on its hands, holding tight
Her Highness's head on the block until the
executioner nuclease, the axeman, arrived.
Time bestowed Queen Jeans with hazy moments
to ponder the provenance that had launched
this disaster.

The cell is a populous precinct with a surplus
of suspects. In such a theater, we must find one
opportune cast member to blame. At that instant,
Queen Jeans trusted that AIF swung the axe like
a guileless guillotine obeying incurious gravity.

PROTEIN PHOBIAS

Packed in a concatenation of atoms,
proteins seem earnest and stern,
the sort of kitchen appliances that would
grind coffee beans or open a beer bottle,
never dissenting from compulsory duties.

Arguably, their nuclear neutrons might
be amenable to upholding the gravitas
of their office, and persuadable protons,
in the end, know their station. But though
their combined nuclear mass dwarfs
the mass of an electron, the nucleus
recoils to a speckle in the vast electron
cloud. Fancy one apple in NYC, the Big
Apple.

We know electrons display passion,
an undeniable fervor, desire, and pride.
They tingle with hopes of initiating intimacy.
In essence, we know that proteins must bridle
their emotions.

Indeed, proteins betray their vehemence
when revealing their phobias. Nostophobia,
the fear of returning home, precludes

erythrocytes, platelets, and white blood cells
from revisiting their birthplace in bone
marrow after their launch. Enochlophobia,
the fear of crowds, keeps DNA in its
gated community, its privileged castle.
Atelophobia, a fear of imperfection,
incites DNA repair enzymes, the most
meticulous, fussbudgety blokes in the cell.

Rare genetic mutations may result
in misfolded proteins that malfunction
or merely act peculiarly.

One marred globin developed nyctophobia,
the fear of darkness, causing him
to flee frantically from the Stygian
bloodstream. An afflicted actin displayed
haphephobia, the fear of being touched,
and this wretched fellow faked his binding
and unbinding to myosin in their cross-bridge
cycle. Alas, limp muscles dangled, undone.
Bruised immunoglobulin G quartets are prone
to lose or gain chains when suffering from
tetraphobia, the fear of the number four.

No pathogenic mutation is more dreaded
by the peptide guild than ebulliophobia,
the fear of bubbles. Enveloped by spherical

lipid bilayers in membranes or vesicles,
the cellmates find no escape hatch to flee
their globular globe.

Succumbing to the vicissitudes of fortune,
mutated proteins rationalize their doom.
Perhaps they've garnered a gain-of-function,
not yet manifest in the prevailing hour.
Consider sickle cell anemia, a ravaging
disease that bestows some benefits
in resistance to malaria.

The Protein Society fiercely debated
this premise, when countless members
developed anthropophobia, the fear
of human beings. This conundrum
caused festering questions to resurface.
Proteins had formerly humored, not feared,
the nebulous outside universe, the human.
But credible rumors attested to a discomforting
reality. When one protein family dies, so, too,
does the human, suggesting, stunningly,
that a human is *alive*. But ... only cell citizens
are alive, or so they thought: "What monstrous
commodity have we wrought? Not a living
entity, surely—for it proves inanimate without us.
Still, might we posit that life could elude us
in the absence of this indifferent godhead?
If we are proven unliving, we were never alive."

PLASTIC-EATING ENZYME

An antibody might like you a little or a lot.
She puckers, crinkles, and scrunches her lips
to grasp you, maybe gingerly, bashfully,
or maybe with lusty suction, precluding escape.
Her kiss might be tardy, though her teeth
squeeze like a python when you venture too close.
Her fringes flutter, affording eclectic contours
and precise stereospecificity.

Antibodies would rather not be enzymes, unless
pressed into service in the technological precincts.
Even then, antibodies half-heartedly remodel their
ligands, with reaction rates far slower than enzymes.
Antibodies are romantics, sophists, ponderers,
stargazers. Antibodies catch, clutch, and conjecture.
Think of Shakespeare's Hamlet holding Yorick's skull.

Enzymes are surgeons. Each ablation or extirpation
proceeds as any other one did. Appendectomy,
tonsillectomy, or biopsy—every cut carves much
like the last. Enzymes don't wish to adapt their
gesticulations to suit their dance partners, as do
antibodies.

When an enzyme is assigned as an escort for one
special man, her partner departs without shoes or hat,
irreparably changed. For better or for worse? She
never knows. Let the fates sort that out. She never
changes a bit when a liaison is over. She works fast,
tailoring countless paramours per second. It never
gets old. She lives for that one fleeting instant
when she and her beau embrace in the transition
state, lowering the energy needed for magic to rise,
existing one wink as a paradisical abstraction.

Two protein families. Two philosophies. Yet
enzymes and antibodies are built from the same
chassis, physique, and contours. Begin with
the multicolored necklace of hundreds of pearls.
Loop up short segments, helices and sheets,
then ball it all up like knitting yarn. Pair up more
yarn balls for complex jobs. Structure determines
function. Thousands of shapes may accrue, and
some prove favorable for achieving a particular
function, with hydrophobic residues inside and
hydrogen bonds stabilizing the mound of angel hair
pasta, with plenty of pockets to harbor the sauce.

Nature has explored every 3D protein fold,
to optimize interactions with cellular playmates.
Proteins, the cellular maestros and gurus,
congenitally exist to be meddlers, though their

substrates feel contented to live and let live.
Surprisingly, their products proffer the same
laissez-faire stance. But Nature instills her
chosen creatures, the biomolecular yarns,
with a compulsion for mingling and manacles.

Nature adapts her best protein folds to
consummate a variety of tasks. Catalytic
triads, commonly found in hydrolases
and transferases, employ three coordinated
amino acid residues, such as S, H, and D,
in the active site. The 3D structure can gather
them closely, even though they're far removed
from each other on the polypeptide necklace.
Nucleophile S donates electrons; H activates S
by acting as the base; D orients H and stabilizes
H's charge during the transition state—minus
a jackpot of majestic details.

Some bacteria learned how to digest
plastics, breaking ester or amide bonds
with revamped enzymes that meticulously
tweaked their vast toolbox of favorable folds.
They fancy plastics were gifted to them,
and no more than they deserve.
The plastic's crumbs proved palatable
morsels, an acquired taste like foie gras,
sushi, Gorgonzola, wabi-sabi, and humility.

KERATIN, FUR, AND FUN

What is Life? Each biomolecule is alive,
or else we are not.

What is consciousness? Regarding a gifted
organism, we say the beast possesses
awareness of itself and its neighborhood.
This conscious thing senses and responds,
or irascibly ignores private and public stimuli.

But consciousness is a private, subjective
insight, an enlightened acquaintance perceiving
something unknowable to another.

Biomolecules respond to stimuli, if in the mood.
They seem to plan ahead, too, anticipating
the next cellular calamity. Biomolecular
consciousness may seem manifest or masked,
but for certain, these entities ponder their world
in trillions of schemes we can't understand.

In the biochemical world, keratin royally ranks
as the most envied adventurer in the cellular
circus. She burst through the barriers imprisoning
most proteins in their black and bloody dungeon.

The alpha-keratin families, coiled, fibrous proteins,
bestow flexibility and durability upon hair. Human
hair is predominately keratin with some sidekicks,
such as melanin that colors the stringy shafts.

As an archetypal outsider, keratin reaches past
boundaries in search of the sublime. In hair, wool,
nails, skin, scales, beaks, claws, and feathers,
find keratin thrusting herself in the apex
of the action. Ever notice your most luscious
locales on your body get the hairiest? I fancy hairs
that pop out in weird places must feel like
a convict digging a tunnel that surfaces in
the prison yard.

In the hair follicle, keratinocyte stem cells make
keratin, then expire, but layers of the keratin
persist in the growing shaft.

Hydrogen bonds within chains fashion
the helical hair strands, which are further
coiled in intermediate fibers, while cross-linked
cysteines stabilize the rods. Hair relaxers
work by breaking these links.

Hair helps a creature keep warm, concoct
camouflage, avoid wounds, and look pretty,
though more motives are embroiled in the intrigue.

Consider the sea otter, the capering clown
on the coasts, who sports the densest fur known
to mammals. They never get cold, and they never
feel on their skin the fluidity of the ocean.

The insulation arises chiefly via a layer of trapped
air next to their hides. The fur is not only dense,
but also spiky and tangled, permitting air to enter
and linger when the otter blows puffs of air
into its well-groomed fur. The dense, furry, and airy
underwear of the otter is topped by longer barbed
guard hairs that repel water.

Keratin peeked her head through the skin, chasing
a dream of flight from all fealty, but decided to make
herself useful in the new workaday world. But, quite
like all proteins, she lives for mirth and for thrills
and for overall merrymaking.

Ever see an otter tobogganing down a snowy hill?
Again and again? Now *whose* idea was *that*!

COLLAGEN: THE ASCETIC

If enzymes are ballerinas, collagens
are the floorboards they dance upon.

Proteins pack personalities within
their squirming balls of yarn. Enzymes
quiver, writhe, wiggle, and tumble,
puckering their pulchritude, swiveling
their lineaments, to break bones
and graft splints on their best friends.

No one knows how proteins gain
temperament or sustain their psyches.
Some say the secret lies in the peptide
bond between amino acids in the chain.
Electrons freewheel between C, N, and O,
the three atoms at the heart of the link,
bestowing a partial double bond flavor
and bolstering greater rigidity in its plane,
than in single C-N bonds.

Electrons appear to change their minds
as they fidget and wander between alternate
haunts. Rumors abound that these flights
of fancy underlie the creation of consciousness
in those boasting a polypeptide pedigree.

I've favored a differing conjecture. A protein's
persona is broadcast by its unique sequence,
the chain of linked amino acid residues.
Take collagen, for example, the protein fiber in
skin, bones, and ligaments. Its iterative sequence
repeats in similar consecutive triplet motifs
of glycine-proline-X, where X varies a bit.

Often, the proline gets hydroxylated to bolster
stability. Individual polypeptide strands form
helices, without any intrachain hydrogen bonding,
thanks to the tiny glycine and constrained
hydroxyproline, which also enable the triple helix
of three collagen strands to form.

Vitamin C enables hydroxylation of collagen
prolines and lysines. Scurvy arises in bodies
bereft of vitamin C.

These lysines get further capped via glycosylation
before the triple helix collagen is exported outside
the cell where it's trimmed and cross-linked
and assembled into collagen fibers that may
be attached to membrane integrins and other
proteins of the extracellular matrix.

Collagens in the skin seem merciful, forgiving,
magnanimous, but bone collagens betray their
stern, stony, and implacable side as these

proteins get mineralized with calcium phosphate
deposits.

Collagen parks as the cell's yogi, celibate,
and monk. Call him the Ascetic. He's traveled
the known world. Now he's at rest, anchored,
though adrift in meditation. He's renounced
the riotous life of an enzyme's bacchanal.
He's frugal, abstinent. He no longer aims
to change anyone's mind but his own. He
seeks not to possess anyone, merely for one
instant's thrill. Resisting temptation, he attains
clarity of thought and inner peace.

Some say he practices the Spiritual Exercises
of St. Ignatius: self-awareness, self-giving,
self-sacrifice, self-understanding. Willing
to suffer for the common good, he's generous.
He's grateful for the miracle of existing at all.
Often free-floating in prayer, he wishes peace
for that madman who encircles his serenity.

Melatonin and the Search for Sleep

Remember Professor Dagonall's Theorem?
"Any proposed signaling pathway requiring
more than three steps … is wrong."

The dizzying JAK/STAT pathway involved
in immune responses and inflammation
meanders from cytokine stimulation,
receptor-ligand activation, phosphorylation,
DNA-binding domains, and transcription
activation. In the end, no one is accountable,
because everyone is to blame. Equivocation
by government bureaucrats seems decisive
in comparison.

The extrinsic pathway of apoptosis,
programmed cell death, employs a
plethora of players to achieve cell suicide,
a brutal yet benevolent slaughter of
community members deemed dangerous
or unnecessary for the precinct's exigent
goals. TNF-alpha, TRAIL, or FasL death
ligands find receptors on the cell's surface.

A signaling complex recruits caspase-8
protease, which activates executioner

caspases that chop up the DNA and protein
pigeons. One might argue that a truly noble
suicide obliges only one molecule or cell
to enact one reckless or reasoned act
of mayhem or martyrdom. Instead, we
view suicide by committee, wherein
the deceased passes away mysteriously,
and no one even recalls what happened.
It's all lost in the haze.

Some say the vindication of Dagonall's
Theorem awaits in our epic quest to unravel
the phenomenon of sleep. What compels us
to sleep? Answer: Every atom in our body
pursues the same sublime sequel—to waft
into slumber, to advance into elsewhere,
where no duties exist, where family and fate
are reordered.

Every brain center avows to seek sleep.
The hypothalamus, thalamus, basal forebrain,
brainstem, amygdala, nucleus accumbens,
substantia nigra, locus coeruleus, and medial
prefrontal cortex—all orchestrate sleep cycles,
the circadian rhythms.

A beloved biomolecule, dopamine, an amino
acid cousin, scouts the brain for nerves already

persuaded that sleep arises at the gateway
to heaven. Strangely, dopamine advocates
for wakefulness, a staid status quo.

Histamine, serotonin, acetylcholine, GABA,
glutamate, adenosine, prostaglandin D_2, and
neuropeptides voice their views on the risks
and rewards of embarking on that dicey voyage
to—*who knows what!* To the utopian faraway!
Every electron intuits and ponders this place.

Professor Dagonall claims that sleep
is inscrutable and the labyrinthine list
of putative patrons and progenitors
confirms that assertion.

That's when an inquisitive molecule,
melatonin, sought to explore Dagonall's
dogma. In truth, he was prodded by a
family member, tryptophan, who agreed
to chronicle his studies. Tryptophan is
both the biggest and rarest of amino acids
found in proteins. He's usually only enlisted
in proteins that seek his planar and hydrophobic
sidecar to anchor in membranes. As a hobby,
he helped synthesize melatonin from his own
used parts, as a lark, to see if he could mess
with the cell's tedious ambience. Since tryptophan,

himself, isn't synthesized in human cells,
he's a worldly chap who has lived other lives
and endured the rigors of food digestion,
which explains his mischievous nature.

Melatonin noticed he was produced in the
brain's pineal gland, mostly at night, then
sailed the bloodstream, willy-nilly, until
bumping into a cell receptor who, seemingly,
was waiting specifically for him. But if no
receptor claims him, in less than an hour's ride,
he'll get digested by the liver.

The cell signaling pathway ignited by him
and his receptor looks like an intergalactic
jigsaw puzzle, with crisscrossing networks,
likely to court chaos. Since he attached to
G protein-coupled receptors, he knew the
action would come fast and furious, with
cAMP fluctuations and kinase phosphorylation
splashing and sputtering.

Tryptophan, who arranged publicity for his pal,
melatonin, spread the word that his client serves
a crucial role in regulating sleep-wake cycles,
plus a dozen other tasks. Professor Dagonall
then did a study that showed melatonin could
be completely removed from the cell—and whatever

organized life that envelops it—while maintaining
a wholly amiable existence for a good long while.

Melatonin felt downcast, knowing he wasn't
essential like his granddad tryptophan.
He thought a lot about sleep, that inner,
outré existence where we shed our allegiances
and brush a new barrier.

KINESIN AND DYNEIN RAILWAY

In a pandemonium of collisions, the cell's
soluble denizens bump and nudge each other.
Call it Brownian motion or brawny
bombardments, most proteins and their
punier pals erratically, half-heartedly,
enact handshakes with anonymous neighbors.

Rarely do lasting friendships arise, except
for the eternal acquaintance with water.
All water molecules look the same
at these blinding speeds, and you never
know which pond imp wets your tush
at any given moment.

We set the thermostat high, and body heat
keeps the players motivated to gyrate
with enough thermal energy to provoke
water sprites to jitter in indecision, never
deciding upon which coordinates to favor
or which boulevard to tour. Proteins pirouette
millions of times every minute and, only by
dumb luck, traverse via diffusion from one
side of the cell to the other.

It's no wonder proteins, guided by divine inspiration, fancied they'd design a mass transit, urban transportation system to ferry folks around the arena, straight as the arrow flies, and with the luxury of travel in high-society comfort.

Hence, the microtubule matrix was assembled, with infinitely more dangling, crisscrossing streamers and balloons than at any rich kid's birthday party.

Unsurprisingly, tubulin protein had lobbied vociferously for his new role in the cytoskeleton. Tubulin, a real backbencher protein that lounged around the cell, was rocketed into princely prestige when assigned to congregate the tubules. Now he could still loaf and drape around the cytoplasm, but in glamor.

The Protein Council had received other proposals for the mass transportation network. Some envisioned a flagellin-propelled submarine. Some proposed an airplane traveling in an expanding vesicle. Some thought a sailboat tugged by chemical gradients might work. But after contentious discourse, the microtubule matrix idea won out.

The Protein Society was charmed by the romance
of railways. Think of it. What makes train travel
intimate, amorous, wistful? In part, one feels
the nostalgia of traversing pathways forged
long before we were born. Moreover, one relishes
the absence of choice in the avenue ordained
for the journey ahead. Someone wiser, this one
glorious instance, made the ideal decision,
and we entrust that we travel to a destination
arranged profoundly for us. Automobile journeys
lack the resoluteness of rails. Air travel and
boating afford infinite thoroughfares, one just
as good as the next. But we all sense there exists
only one *best* way, and railways pledge that the
finest artery awaits.

Repeating units of alpha-beta tubulin heterodimers
assembled into filaments, then into microtubules,
to lay down the railroad tracks. Two principal
locomotives, dynein and kinesin, were invented,
both with boxcars to ferry their riders and cargo.

Both locomotives harvest the energy derived
from hydrolysis of ATP fuel to power their motors.
Flooding a cell in millimolar amounts, the ATPs
preen like matches howling to be lit.

Dynein can lug massive cargo—vesicles, organelles, transcription factors, ribonucleoprotein complexes, and aggregated proteins. As the dynein subunits undergo conformational changes when prodded by ATP's ignition, dynein appears to walk along the microtubule cable by alternating firm and weak tractions on its two feet.

Cartoons depict a bumpy ride, more like a horse and buggy than a train, but locals who have boarded the train cars assert that it's the smoothest ride you can ever get with your clothes on. Dynein ferries cargo from the cell periphery toward the cell center, whereas the other motor protein, kinesin, transports its passengers on the opposite route. Few riders book a ticket for the return trip.

Kinesin cornered the cell market for ferrying vesicles between the endoplasmic reticulum and the Golgi complex. Kinesin moves a bit slower than dynein, especially when ATP levels dwindle, but kinesin can lug larger payloads. Globular proteins in the cell relentlessly mock motor proteins for their gangly appearance. Their balloon heads and stork legs make them look like a stop sign, or like a toad on a lily pad, or like a basketball balanced on a golf club.

But height matters, and these guys
are sure tall enough to see the flashing,
clanging red lights at the end of the tracks.

Disillusionment descended on The Protein Council
when they realized dynein and kinesin had gotten
too big for their britches. The two locomotives
were only interested in carrying celebrity customers,
local dignitaries, and cytoplasmic socialites,
traveling to oversee spindle formation,
chromosome alignments, or nerve axon signaling.

The protein peasants in the cytoplasm
were never offered a ride on the fancy monorail.
As they randomly tumbled in the cellular soup,
sometimes bouncing off the microtubule cables,
they never knew that in the big top, outside them,
it works the same way.

MITOSIS DISTRIBUTION

Hereabouts, walls are like windows.
That thing passing through
is untouchable, abstract, ethereal,
something imagined from paltry evidence,
but theatrical emotions.

Call me Mr. Bow Tie.

Or call me connexin, possibly the prettiest
protein in the cell. With my twin alpha-helical
wings and central beta sheet knot,
friends say I resemble a bow tie.
Enemies call me a noose. I create
the tunnel between bordering cells.

My twelve identical chains perforate
the adjacent membranes of neighboring
cells, with six of us stationed in each bordering
cell, sewing ourselves inside with four stitches.

We're specialists in channel building
and create gap junctions connecting
the cytoplasm of bumping cells, thereby
allowing intercellular communication, so I'm told.
I welcome tourists, ions, and species I cannot
name. I presume they carry a vital message
or perhaps idle gossip. Who's to judge?

Not a glamorous job. The action happens
downstream, even though I'm the key player.
Lounging around the membrane affords me
ample, overly abundant, time to brood upon
and intuit the nature of surfaces:

Love poses upon surfaces, upon turf,
upon a frozen pond. Love strolls the bridge
over the gorge. Love's yacht plows upon
the surface of the sea, not its interior.
One day, the ship's bow probes too deeply
and discovers the grand abyss of emotion.

My channel lies in cardiac muscle
and coordinates the heart's contractions.

Most proteins I've met evince suspicion,
qualms, even mistrust concerning my job.
They love walls. They love privacy and would
build walls inside walls, if they could. They'd
board up my windows, if they could. Surfaces
safeguard us from the dire enigma out there,
an unknown peril imparting impermanence.

Although the adult heart typically grows
by enlarging its existing cells, I heard that
a mitosis festival got scheduled for today.
Interphase had completed its work, always
a furtive process behind nuclear curtains.

DNA replication transpired and sister
chromatids, bound by a centromere, arrived.
Now, each chromosome copy awaited a wall.

The main event proves the crowd pleaser
every time. It never gets old. Chromosomes
condense. The nuclear membrane dissolves.
Then spindle microtubules get erected
to haul DNA cargo to preassigned seats
along the equator of the cell. The spindle pulls
the chromosomes to opposite poles so each
daughter cell gets an identical set of forty-six
before the nuclear membranes reform.

I should feel awe about it, but, unfortunately,
life is too awesome to feel anything, except
for one ephemeral instant, when you forget
that it's even possible.

For me, the exciting part is cytokinesis, a physical
division of the cytoplasm into two daughter cells.
An actin-myosin contractile ring pinches the cell
membrane's middle until the cleavage is completed.
All of the cell soup, including the mitochondria,
need to get divided equally.

Most divorces partition the property and assets
equally, though not necessarily equitably between
spouses, and horse trading often occurs. I could tell

monstrous tales of the bickering and brawling that erupts between daughter cells before the bisecting wall finally closes, and well beyond that.

I guess the root problem is DNA's paradigm, the high bar set from DNA's established precedent. When DNA replicates, its sister strands prove to be identical, right down to the last base. But in the extramural world in the cytoplasm, and realms beyond, nothing gets equally divided. Every entity is distinct, with only the contrivance of equity to comfort the moralist. You can't split a pizza in half. One half has a bit more mozzarella, a bit less sauce. A half sandwich has more or less mayonnaise than its mated half hoagie.

Before the cytokinesis rung down the curtain, the daughter cells caterwauled liked alley cats, accusing each other of hogging the ribosomes, snatching the newest proteins, double-dipping in the salty soup to procure a more voluminous pool.

Some protein agitators took sides, questioning their placements in one or the other of the daughter cells, propounding some rationale for why one village bested the other. Unscrupulous proteins lugged tiny handfuls of cytoplasmic brine to overfill the pool in their favored cellular home. One gang

hijacked a mitochondrion, in a madcap dash to
the border before the gate closed forevermore.

It was chaos. But strangely, when the hatch and
double door finally fused and sealed, the finale
fell soundlessly, and then silence felt foreboding,
ominous, unsettling, as though a grievous mistake
had occurred, though we would never know what.

I only knew I, Mr. Bow Tie, would soon be summoned
to drill another channel in the wall, wherein rumors
of paramount affairs are ferried through my own
promiscuous pores. I take time to peruse the pastures
on both sides of the fence. Some minutes, I detect
distinctness in these neighboring burgs, though
a clement glance reacquaints me with their kindred
complexions.

If asked, I respond, "They're alike.
Each outlook differs."
A wall crafts an elusive dimension.

Nerve Storm of GABA

Find me, GABA, at Lover's Leap.

Nerve cells improvise their own standard
of beauty. Outsiders err in viewing cells
in visible light, rather than conceiving
them in darkness. Shine a spotlight
upon a nerve cell and lay bare an unearthly
monstrosity. Fancy your detached hairy head
directly attached to one of your arms with your
fingers wagging genially. Nothing more.
Your head is the nerve cell body. Your scalp
hair portrays dendrites. Your arm impersonates
an axon.

As with any cell, the esthetics and allure
prevail in the thousands of proteins inside,
piloting this fairylike ferry. The neuron crew
transmits electrical and chemical signals.
Rumors suggest the billions of brain neurons
can form countless trillions of connections,
enabling vast vats of stored gossip. Supposedly,
the ultimate processing decisions arise
in a communal consensus, though in practice,
some neurons eschew equitable principles.

The brain conveys enough electrical power
to turn on a flashlight, though nerves never
intentionally search for anything in the dark.
Electrical impulses move at several hundred
miles per hour, not that fast by most molecular
standards, but nerves run a tangled and ticklish
shop. They're a greasy lot, but thank goodness
for the fatty myelin sheath wrapping each neuron,
insulating nerve fibers, and quickening nerve
impulses.

Axons, the neurons' lanky wires, transmit
electrical messages away from the cell body,
whereas dendrites, those frizzy threads on
the neuron, receive transmitted signals from
another neuron's axon. Each neuron is a
merchant, a trader, an envoy, buying and selling
goods at prices putatively fixed, though each
neuron might place its thumb on the scales.
Who would know? They never tattle on a crony.

The real excitement, big thrills, and flamboyant
fireworks abound at the synapses, the tiny gaps
between the tips of the axon and the dendrite.
Chemical messengers leap from axon to dendrite,
like trapeze performers launched in midair, and
the recipient neuron hurls new electrical signals
down its axon as the process repeats. Electrical

current arises from transient flows of sodium and
potassium ions across neuron membranes.

It's amazing, of course, but a standard drill that can
seem mundane and monotonous. But then, I am
a traffic cop, a bridge builder, a synapse stevedore,
and I'm too fatigued by tingles that the axon parades
to be an impartial observer. Maybe the most stunning
thing about life is that it quickly becomes wholly
believable, and no more than we deserve.

Perhaps something I did helped control a heart rate,
or digestion, or breathing. I never found out.
It might be that I help someone feel pain
or contemplate the cause.

I wouldn't care, if I knew. My gang and I agree
to the leap for the love of the quest, for the thrill
of the hunt. After a dreary pontoon ride inside
a neuron's synaptic vesicle, we neurotransmitters
are released when the electric current reaches
the axon terminal tip, and we float freely,
diffusing across the crack, the crevasse,
the cleft, perhaps then binding to receptors
on the neighboring neuron, who might regard
the event as a meaningful message.

Call me GABA, gamma-aminobutyric acid.
I was created with a mission in mind

and boast a brain-born pedigree. The enzyme
glutamate decarboxylase synthesized me
from glutamate, using vitamin B6 to pull
off the job. Some glutamates, the key excitatory
neurotransmitters, were inciting such a free-for-all
frenzy in this precinct that I was created as
his counterpart, the key inhibitory messenger
in synaptic milieus. I'm an Eve to his Adam.

I notice I seem to tamp down the electrical
currents in the next town, so maybe it's working.
Don't bother thanking me for calming your anxiety
or fears. I'm always upbeat and can't comprehend
your mood swings.

I only wish you could freefall with me on
that majestic voyage between neurons,
those moments of nonpareil liberty and
absurd expectations. In that interim, I wish
to remain unencumbered forever, though
I seek the burden of love. Maybe I will
diffuse blissfully away in the syrup. Maybe
my lover receptor will embrace me, and
an ecstatic pain will lurch me to passions
unknown.

And what then? Maybe I will undergo
reuptake into the neuron I vacated. Maybe

I'll meet my assassin. Maybe I'll be invited
into neighboring brain glia cells.

There's never a finale, only an intermission,
in the hippocampal hippodrome, or in any
cellular playhouse.

We neurotransmitters relish our family ties,
not just glutamate and me, but also dopamine,
histamine, serotonin, norepinephrine, and glycine.
We're all amino acids or descendants of them.
Tryptophan, tyrosine, and histidine sowed more
wild oats than a dandelion farm. We could've
joined the conga line of amino acids in protein
chains, but something wild in our soul incited
us to go it alone.

On my voyage, in the void between neurons,
I marvel at the beauty of the integral membrane
proteins, especially each four-helix bundle
of chains that span the lipid layer of the
membrane, with hydrophobic amino acid
residues embedded within the greasy bilayer.

I wonder whether the enveloping fats
coerce the coiled proteins to curl up
that way in their elegant pose. Maybe all
those proteins wish to be carefree, slovenly
threads undulating in the ether, but the cell's

encroaching milieu casts them as voluptuous
vixens.

Maybe all this was done,
the crossfire and confetti,
just to create me.

MEMORY WHODUNIT

We are our memories.
We recall our identity.
We discover a nonpareil self.
Mark me Protein Incognito.
At the moment, I can't quite
recall how I augmented your
memory. Remembrance is
a knotty affair, and every
polymer and punk in our neuron
was awarded an assignment in
one phase of the game.

As a thought too timeworn to be true,
a memory recalls something
that never happened that way.
Thank me for massaging the data
in your diary.

I, Protein Incognito, recall only
my molecular mission, despite all
the community service I've rendered
to the enveloping entity I don't
understand. Neither do any of my
colleagues in this odd enterprise.

Mistrustful of memories, I only recollect
my choreography, the sequence of steps
as I fold in my 3D structure, marking
the margins of my molecular dynamics,
the quirky dance I rerun as I pirouette
in the cell.

Maybe your memory resembles mine.
I seek to fold into a pose that achieves
a global minimum of Gibbs free energy,
either decreasing enthalpy or increasing
entropy. Thermodynamics dictates that I
release energy by folding with advantageous
hydrogen bonds, van der Waals forces,
and ionic interactions while also releasing
water molecules to meander freely.
My memory proves impressive in fulfilling
these duties.

As denizens of a hippocampal neuron,
we biomolecules were pressed into service
to the mysterious leviathan we colonize.
Our task was to achieve long-term
potentiation of its memories, assisting
this colossus in remembering some
rather meaningless drivel. Every player
on the stage changed something in
the cell. Some merely rearranged

the furniture, but you're not allowed
to do nothing. At least, act like you're
busy. I worked with the synapse crew,
pumping out frisky neurotransmitters
across the gap between my tingling
neuron's axon tip and the dozing neuron
next door, where another crew was
erecting more dendritic receptors to
strengthen the signaling transfers.

My guys could sense the calcium flux
that ripped open vesicles where the
glutamate messengers were stored.
I heard the action potentials fire and hum
like a festival's fireworks, so I guess
the big guy was thinking hard about
something.

I never saw so many dendrites sprouting
on my own cell before, like a toupee on
a guy with male-pattern baldness. Pretty soon,
the whole neighborhood started gossiping
about news we didn't even fathom. You
don't really get impressed by the duality
of a neuron until it ramps up, full blast.
Neurons are both pitchers and catchers
of signaling chemicals. Each neuron is
a one-armed axon pitcher, but a multiarmed

dendritic catcher, though even axons branch
into multiple terminals. Imagine the assembly.
Think of a spider web or snowflake, a maze
of liaisons. Every neuron engenders thousands
of connections in the network.

Before long, we had the whole town
chanting this one idea, even if it was
mostly untrue. You might get the impression
that all these neurons agreed on the same
basic concept right from the start, and that
made it easy to form a cohesive community.
Really, though, it's usually one loudmouth
who gets the ball rolling, and the rest
follow along.

While I was busy busting synaptic vesicles
and spilling neurotransmitters into
the pond bordering neighboring neurons,
every other molecular artisan in our arena
did their part to make our messaging durable.

You know DNA would stick her big nose into it
and trigger gene transcription to call in
the cavalry, though some tasks don't require
her input. Key kinase enzymes perform
phosphorylation of glutamate receptors, like
AMPA, elevating their surface abundance in

the recipient cell, thereby promoting excitatory
activity. Some transcription factors, such as
CREB, get in on the act. New scaffolding gets
erected in the recipient neuron using PSD-95
and Homer1c to stabilize the top-heavy synapse.
Anonymous proteins like me, Protein Incognito,
increase the dendritic spine numbers and density,
synaptic vesicle number, and sensitivity to
neurotransmitters.

Biology usually interposes buffers to keep
the factories from exploding. You'll guess
something constrains our exuberance in
exploiting synaptic plasticity to the point
of ignition. Confidentially, ghost messengers
sneak back from the stimulated neuron
to hose down the hothead that sent them
the signal. I've witnessed these ghosts waft
in the dark across the synapse, smelled
them for sure. Not saying I'm one. Some say
they're endocannabinoids, or nitric oxide,
or BDNF. I can smell 'em, and I say they ain't.
But maybe I'm wrong. I usually am. Except
about me.

Biomolecules perceive that only we understand
consciousness, but we can't fathom memories,
not the ones the leviathan endures. Still, when

asked, we'll deliver an answer. Blame us,
if you wish, when your memories torment you.
Find solace in knowing, we never divulge
a diary's redactions.

THALAMUS TALES

Ever wonder why you never learn
the important stuff? Well, you can blame
the shop where I work with a bunch
of mindless bureaucrats, myself excluded.

They tell me my office squats squarely at the brain's
dead center, no aspersion intended, all the better
to serve as the central relay station for the brain's
memory. My agency, the thalamus, filters and
outrageously edits our appraisals of sight, touch,
and sound.

Another bureau handles smells, I don't know
why, and I guess there's a funny story buried
in there that I'll let you figure out. Sensory data
dispatched from the optic nerve or from HQ
downstairs in the brainstem gets mailed up here
to our switchboard to get so severely redacted
and fudged that neither the cerebral cortex
nor you will ever guess what the original sender
was trying to say.

I'll need to present my credentials, not that you'd
care, but credentials are the coin of the realm in
my shop. We erase all considerations of merit

in our edited documents. Indeed, the M-word is
never spoken by us. Folks call me GABAAR,
and I'm a senior deputy in charge of mediating
inhibition of information transfer.

We tell the public that it's in their best interest.
After all, if you paid attention to every trivial
sight, sound, or sensation, you'd go nuts.
There's too much information, and we'll decide
for you what's important. In reality—well, I overuse
that word—we keep you from experiencing reality.

I, GABAAR, am a ligand-gated ion channel, and
I shut down neurotransmission by pouring chloride
ions into neurons, which inhibits their electrical
firings. The neurotransmitter GABA tried to grab
the spotlight, but I'm the force who gets the job
done as a transmembrane pentameric receptor
who controls the plug in the pore.

It's a clannish place here in the thalamus,
fantastically different from the rest of the brain.
We call it the thalamic reticular nucleus here
where I hang my hat, though I sometimes
exchange views with the basal ganglia crowd
and the drama queens in the amygdala.
We think of ourselves as the gatekeepers, the
middlemen, the stoplights that pause, then purify,
the sensory signals that bombard our nerve network.

I pity the frontline sensory receptors in eyes or ears
that transduce physical stimuli by triggering changes
in membrane potential, provoking an electrical signal.
Sodium ions rush into a sequence of channels,
bestowing a self-propagating nerve impulse, before
potassium ions rush out and tranquility returns.

Those guys wouldn't believe what we do to their
reports before we send our version to the cerebral
cortex. We decide what's important and what you
should ignore. One of the guys has a poster on
his office wall: "The Power to Ignore."
It's our motto, and I won't let the team down.

While I'm guessing my own role is pretty
important in censoring the news, we in
the thalamus precincts don't entirely know
how all the neural connections get unplugged.
Everything gets jumbled. I know there's a bunch
of transcription factors that are overexpressed
in our neurons. Our town almost looks like
a foreign locale, some days, and I'm nearly
afraid to say hi to the strangers in town.

Who even knows what these growth factors
and calcium-binding proteins do around here?
Some say a circuit linking the thalamus to
the cerebral cortex regulates perceptions

of consciousness, but, if so, we persistently
leave out the best parts in the story, on our side.
Sometimes, we'll get messages back from
the cortex imploring us to shut down messages
about their health so they can focus on watching
a ballgame, and we're happy to oblige if we're
in the mood to be helpful.

If we're not in the mood and shirk our duty,
HQ tells us that folks start to engage in much
more creative thinking. Without us filtering
the news, the unbiased information about
the real world causes folks to integrate
disparate ideas and produce novel concepts.

Naturally, that admonition shames us into
regarding the gravity of our assignments.
We presume this entity we govern, this
rumored leviathan we advise, cannot stomach
the truth, could not maneuver a realm so
antithetical to the fantasies it relishes.

Furthermore, we frankly feel our grip upon
truth surpasses whatever the leviathan
imagines could rise to the rims of importance.
Therefore, we tell "It" what *ought* to be true,
never what *is* true. It, this thing, smiles at our
artful portrait of reality. The contortion feels
agreeable, almost pleasant. We withhold

awareness, and the congenial imposture
that It perceives will empower It to flourish
as a flawed theoretician.

A random and comprehensive exposure
to information would render It impotent.
What if actual facts barged through Its brain?
It could no longer nurture deceptions
of peace, justice, and equity. What if It
no longer feared censure for speaking
the truth? What if It weighed decisions
with raw rationality? This must not happen.
Not on our watch.

It, our protégé and figurehead king,
lives in a celebrity world. The deaths
of thousands of neighbors, the suffering
of millions of countrymen, never happened.
Only today's news of the divorce of some
movie star grazes Its thoughts. One
glamorous event embodies the aggregate
of all sensory input.

I knew we'd failed in our mission.
We'd hoped to trim, prune, peel,
and strip sensory input, flake by flake,
until no remnant remained, announcing
the quintessence of consciousness
that It might apprehend and embrace.

BRAIN JANITOR

Success basks in fellowship.
Failure broods, fatherless.

I, TREM2, reside on the brain's microglia,
the skull meat's immune cells that act
as janitor, ambulance corps, and coroner,
tasked with the clearance of neuronal
wreckage.

Microglia are shape-shifting cells that thrust
an array of tentacles about the cerebrospinal
fluid, CSF, where we sail in the brain's ventricles.
Microglia are nosey, always checking up
on the health of nearby neurons. We fancy
we're compassionate, cleaning up cellular debris
and dead or dying cells before they can build up
and cause damage, maybe dementia.

I enjoy cruising our microglia hearse in the CSF,
though the central parenchyma is our headquarters.
We don't notice the darkness. The hum of the brain
guides our ship. I love the night shift. Maybe it's
the graveyard shift, from our clientele's perspective.
Drifting along, always on the edge of life and death,
bestows a sense of grandeur you only understand
if you experience it.

Microglia engulf and digest cellular trash, misfolded
protein aggregates, defunct synapses, and bacterial
invaders. Any act of phagocytosis feels solemn,
as though we swallowed the enigma of life.

A transmembrane protein, I, TREM2, flaunt a
gorgeous beta sheet structure admired by my
peers on the microglia cell surface. I can bind
to a variety of ligands, mostly glycoproteins
and lipids, and my choke holds alert my colleagues
inside the cell to complete our janitorial work.
The signaling pathways are complex, but each
player imagines she is the one responsible for
our success. And so do I. Without me, the factory
shuts down, or so I am told by objective observers.
When microglia fail in their mission,
Alzheimer's disease may develop.

My patrol boat cleared out a bunch of amyloid
plaques in the past hour. Who knows whether
this gesture mattered in the grand scheme
of things, but it's fun to do it, and that's what
matters to me. I sometimes listen to the factory
noise below in our cell. It sounds strange,
an industrious sound, maybe from the sparks
of ATP matches igniting. Sometimes, I seem to
smell something down there, an alien smell,
as though my own home were a faraway jungle,

and the endless river of brain fluids bequeathed
my true domicile.

Indeed, to my delight, I know not whether I sail
on a river, a lake, or a sea. But on the shorelines,
always, I hear the murmurs of new thoughts,
the sizzles of synapses throbbing, the purr
of reminiscences drifting to sleep for a season.

Which memories will never reawaken?
What perceptions had perished in my
seafaring hearse? My crew erases the past,
the once vibrant yesterdays. Antiquity
expired. Only hearsay, rumors, and gossip
will be recorded to chronicle some semblance
of each flamboyant thought.

I handle with care each tumbledown neuron
we bury. We afford one last flicker
of dignity before its entrance
into the contortion of history.

CONUNDRUM OF CONSCIOUSNESS

Last week, a brouhaha bubbled
in the neuroscience community,
when Sniffit-Jarkshart mathematics
and grain-drive biophysics confirmed
key postulates of "innate consciousness."

The whole affair began when unusually
long RNA molecules—modified with
unorthodox chemical moieties and folded
in contorted, dynamic shapes—were
discovered in human embryos. These RNA
strands crumbled and vanished at about
the time when the first fetal neurons appeared,
around day forty or so.

Moreover, a strange electromagnetic flux
pulsed in the early fetus, bustling with
inscrutable electric field intensity and
inexplicable magnetic field strength.
The bewildering event gradually transfigured
into stable electromagnetism, about six weeks
post-pregnancy.

Professors Sniffit and Jarkshart proposed
that innate consciousness exists at human

conception—then undergoes adulteration and attenuation as the naive, fetal neural network begins its clumsy attempts to make sense of this bizarre new existence.

Innate consciousness never disappears. But an emerging pseudo-consciousness from the nervous system muddles the inborn messages, as both real and sham consciousness compete for attention.

Hence, Drs. Sniffit and Jarkshart launched an upheaval among the research community. The two investigators asserted that a human's neuron-spawned consciousness presents itself as an imp to be vanquished, rather than a sprite to be fostered. In hindsight, it seemed obvious to them that consciousness could not be explained by contemporary knowledge of the foibles of nerves.

"Counterfeit consciousness," a byname also attributed to Sniffit and Jarkshart, arose as a leading field of inquiry, especially among young investigators who sensed their former enlightenment but feared they were getting dumber each day.

Scholars now faced a daunting, maybe insurmountable, hurdle in unraveling this matter. On the one hand, nerves remain indispensable to thriving in life. On the other hand, the recognition of "ersatz awareness," another Sniffit-Jarkshart idiom, compelled them to put forth remedial reasonings.

But where to begin in a nerve's electrical, chemical, and mechanical signaling?

Nerve signals lack the simplicity of the Morse code, though similarities are noted. Patterned signals are employed by both, and the dots and dashes of Morse might be paired with the quick fluctuations in voltage along nerve cells. Morse uses on or off states, though, whereas nerves display an incessant sweep of voltage shifts.

The rate at which nerve signals spike can bestow alternate messages. The duration, strength, and arrangement of these spikes afford a plethora of possible data transmissions.

Both chemical and electrical signals may vary in velocity and potency. Distinct neurons relay distinct types of signals, and the breadth of myelin coatings affects transmission speed.

Nerve signals usually move fast, maybe as fast
as a jogger or a racecar. But these messages
go slowly compared to electricity that travels
near the speed of light. The movements of
ions across neuron membranes, and possibly
the transient mechanical forces, limit velocities.

Once a neuron's voltage commits to a spike,
each signal goes full blast, though frequency
of spikes vary. The mists of released
neurotransmitters differ, and the receptor
types on the receiving neuron vacillate.

None of this explains consciousness.
But it may explain what confounds our
faulty subjective awareness of the world
based on subjective experiences. Adult
brains enjoy abstract thinking, solving
pseudo-problems, and planning pseudo-
events. An embryo, maybe even a fetus,
knows something we forgot. Later, the hapless
tyke must cope with our mundane milieu
of earthly existence for a while.

During pregnancy, the youngster's
environment, the liquid meals,
the stressful confinement in a
cramped hammock, the spurious

toxins and noise, all pester and provoke her to vexation.

The fetal brain displays amazing plasticity. The spinal cord's first synapses form by week seven, and then begin to sprout all around her anatomy. The brain starts to modify existing connections and creates new synaptic pathways, rewiring the motherboard, halfway forgetting the fundamental stuff.

Professors Sniffit and Jarkshart refocused their laboratories on embryology, in unfunded research at an undisclosed location, seeking the kernel of consciousness suffusing an immaculate cell.

PART III:

divine biochemistry

THE UNANSWERED QUESTION

So, this guy said to me, "What's that noise?"

Like any vitamin B12 introvert, I try to keep
a low profile in the cell. I usually can, except
when there's another screwup in DNA
methylation, and, naturally, they'll blame
the most remote parts dealer, namely me.

I've been a cofactor for methionine synthetase
since the invention of tools, and I rarely
make a mistake that could mess up DNA
methylations at all. If anyone gets sassy
about it, I first off tell them to call me
"cobalamin," since most of my detractors
don't even know I carry a cobalt ion in my
back pocket, and that puts them on the defensive
right away, 'cause they know I got some smarts.

That's why I got caught napping when this
guy asked, "What's that noise?" instead
of accusing me of malfeasance.

I could tell this dope looked like a transfer RNA,
just a little tyke in a trefoil shape with the two
ends of his RNA chain near each other in a
protuberance. Being a tRNA, he sported

some exotic base modifications, of course,
plus an anticodon, to please the mRNA.
But this guy looked to be an initiator
methionine tRNA. No wonder he was confused.
He's supposed to lay down the first amino acid
in a protein chain. It's a lonely job because
you never know if you'll get any followers.

Those tRNA freaks fancy they're both
nucleic acid and protein, and they'll never
admit they're neither one. You get a lot
of platonic preaching from these guys,
usually, but they don't care about any other
biomolecule, and, to be honest, neither do I.
It's wholly about the thrill of the moment
down here, and that's enough for anyone.

I'm guessing this guy singled me out for
that inquiry because, frankly, I've been around,
a pretty worldly bloke. I'm not a hometown
boy and can't be synthesized in the local
factory here. Having once been meat, in a
past life, bestows a quirky aura around me
with the neighbors, so I've discovered.
Besides, I'm the largest vitamin, and height
affords some air of wisdom. I don't know why.

Anyway, when this guy asked, "What's that noise?"
I told him, "You mean that background hum? It's
just the stretching of chemical bonds. *Hey*, are you
new 'round here? I got used to that my second day."
And he said, "No, I don't mean the faint squeal of
chemical bonds oscillating. I mean that intermittent
thunder. You can hear it best near a membrane.
To me, it sounds like, 'Lub-Dub. Lub-Dub.'"

Well, *I* sure never heard that, and I knew this guy
was a nut. So, I whipped out a brochure I designed
for wackos like him. "Here's a map of the cell. See
if you can track down the source of that sound."
It wasn't a real map of the cell, of course, which
would need to get edited each instant, but I knew
he'd spend a lifetime racing down blind alleys,
and I'd never get bothered by him again.

Better still, he'd hear lots of noise every moment,
but only when he'd get really close to the cell's big
machines, like the replisome, the transcriptional
pulleys and gears, and the spliceosome. I presumed
this guy had ridden on the ribosome roller coaster
so many times that he didn't even notice the clangor
and clatter and rattle and racket of the mRNA
and nascent polypeptide chains slapping the chassis
of the macromolecular monstrosity.

Sound waves travel faster and maintain their energy longer in aqueous precincts compared to air, and I envisioned this guy swimming toward each fleeting flash of noise, never knowing from whence it came. I guess that sounds mean, and maybe I am, but it's nothing compared to the racket I endured while being chewed as an imp in a porkchop or riding flatulence avalanches in the small intestine.

By some crazy coincidence, I bumped into this tRNA again, hours later. He'd jettisoned his old methionine, which launched the sprouting stem of some protein. Now he'd packed on a new methionine, which he'll squander as impulsively and recklessly as the last one. He never knew what protein he's making. He just waved his wand and they start stringing a sequence, or so he said. Random diffusion cast us together near the cell membrane, and, just then, I got a scare. "Lub-Dub. Lub-Dub." That's how it sounds.

"Wow! You were right," I said to the tRNA. "Huh? About what?" he replied. "Can't you hear that noise?" I said. "Um, no, not really," he said, "just background buzz, the flutter of the wings, the breath of a fairy, the hiss of a million bursting bubbles in the froth, winking away, one by one by one."

In a moment of fluster and flurry, I brooded
on the possibility that I, myself, created
the sound—or perhaps I and the billions
of the cellular water molecules splashing.
Raindrops sound like distant drummers.

I attempted to swing my frame to
amplify their collisions, but the tRNA's
insight proved prescient. I could not
replicate the ghostly sound that I'd heard.

"Something's out there," I spoke to no one now.

"Who are you?" I regretted my puny voice
the moment I perceived its whimper. I had
asked the wrong question. Not the inquiry
that discomfits the cellular settlers.

"Why?"

"Why?"

The hum, never a silence, brushes your
cheeks, passes by, evinces no awareness
of you, until the chosen time.

ABSCISSION

Leafy locals call me "Auxin, the Aloof."

To the contrary, I patrol as the most
passionate sentry in the floral domains.

When autumn gusts rustle a maple
tree's mane, one leaf at a time springs
into flight, never two together. Each
commands its brief gala in time.

Leaves aggrandize that word, leaving
as every sentient creature should do,
ruling the air for one ethereal episode,
soaring, pirouetting, splashing its red
tincture across the gaseous canvas,
striping a mural upon a vanishing veneer,
painting a parable of the concatenation
of a life, lived one wave at a time,
each instant so brief that the scene
affixes the frontiers of nothing.

The scarlet leaf lands on the pavement,
face up, more beautiful in death
than in life, browbeating an observer
into pondering personhood.

Few things excite me. This is one.

I employed the tools available.
If I owned a magic wand, the spectacle
might seem more bewitching only to
those not rapt by esthetic pursuits.

Abscission, an onomatopoeic word,
transpires when a tree drops a leaf,
often in autumn, judging its immediate
utility as groundless.

The leaf's chlorophyll is scavenged,
and green disappears, whereas carotenoids
and anthocyanins degrade slower, and so
do their warm, vibrant orange-yellow-reds.

At the abscission site, cork cells create
a tough and waterproof layer to seal
the wound when the unfurled, flamboyant
flag leaps to its paradisical plunge.

Enzymatic assailants or water engorgements
execute the final, irrevocable severance.

Two plant hormones, one vainglorious,
one gaseous, ignited this frenzy. I, Auxin,
the Aloof, am the former. Ethylene is the latter.

In candor, my power lies in my absence.
I'm tasked with preventing the formation
of the abscission zone's cast of players.
No theater, no drama, no spectacle twinkles
there whenever I'm policing the grounds.
But I'm a scofflaw at heart, a perhaps too
bighearted dreamer who slinks from his post,
knowing majestic mayhem will detonate.
As my concentration dwindles at the docketed
abscission zone site, my sidekick, ethylene,
can saunter mainstage and mysteriously
incite gene expression of cellulase and other
cell wall-wrecking enzymes.

Ethylene and I turn out to be distant cousins.
We both have grandads who labored in proteins.
My forebear was tryptophan, an unwieldy klutz
whose prodigious girth makes him the go-to guy
to fill in a hole. With time on his hands, with no
pits to presently plug, he tinkered around and
invented me, a petite ghost of himself, but sporting
our signature flat-as-a-pancake indole ring.

Ethylene descended from methionine, an amino
acid rather sparsely employed in plant proteins.
Methionine dreamed of flight, just like me, and
his invention of a gaseous avatar for himself
still gets celebrated on a major plant holiday
and also whenever fruit ripens.

Ethylene and I, the Aloof, are jack-of-all-trades,
actually, though we don't brag about it anymore,
nor any less. Transmembrane gasoreceptors
recognize ethylene's slightly sweet scent or
minimalist contours, then swing into signaling.

I, the Aloof, whip up gene expression—or shut
it down—by devious devices. Some auxin receptors
are named F-box proteins; they target selected
proteins for degradation via ubiquitin tagging.
I partner with ubiquitin ligase to pinpoint those
proteins confounding my schemes. Their death in
the proteasome is a grisly, though deserving, demise.
Don't let those with an artistic disposition fool you.
Artists are the most violent beasts in any herd.
If a protein gets in the way of my poetic vision,
I arrange their brutal destruction. No time for
persuasion. The ultimate flight of the foliage
condones any transgression. The beauty justifies
the barbarity.

I've slept in ancient papyrus scrolls,
among archives of the Redeemer,
proclaiming, "Store up for yourselves
treasures in heaven."

I've dwelled in woody papers decreeing,
"Faith is the assurance of things hoped for,
the conviction of things not seen."

When each leaf leaps, my own
manifestation absconds. I'm disaffiliated.

I enter the breach. Dangling in delirium.
Twirling, diving, up-floating, rolling,
skittering, tumbling, gliding, sliding,
I, the Aloof, attain the divinity of the nothing.
"And nothing will be impossible to you."

Enzymes: Militant Maniacs

The body's molecular machines, enzymes,
feature copious quavering countenances,
as exquisitely expressive as human faces.

In their dynamic crevices and proboscises,
fancy you spy three pairs of eyes
and four wagging tongues licking

a comrade, a taste that might portend
a swallow or a nudge, instigating
ecstasy somewhere in the network trenches.

All enzymes are trembling skeletons,
though they appear to sprout faces.
Their passionate visages manifest

a mission. Yet each protein prevaricates,
equivocates, thrusting a new pose, then
quickly retrieving her former shape,

as if nothing happened, even though
she bit off her coworker's nose. What's more,
she intends to do it again to a hundred more

collegial confidantes in less than a second.
An incendiary catalyst, the enzyme incites
a cataclysmic change and walks away unscathed

and indifferent. These protein provocateurs
act as outlaws, when adjudged in the perspective
of our society's slant. We measure meters,

while the tiny agitators survey nanometers.
In this divine dimension, ethics undulate
at a pitch misheard by the mind.

MEMBRANE WALLS

We love surfaces. We erect walls.
My home, my fortress, bestows
only one door. As gatekeeper,
I limit access. All who pass
the door acknowledge my rules.

A cell membrane, like a halo,
unfurls a spherical surface.
A bilayer of lipids chart and uphold
the neighborhood. Like an exotic
soap bubble, with arcades inside,

the cell membrane boundary
serves the whimsy of the nuclear boss,
a unique chieftain with eccentric goals.
But too many doors rattle on the slippery orb,
the grandiose globule, the everywhere border,

and gullible doormen sometimes grant entry
to outlaws, past thousands of gateways,
from hundreds of hatches. The border
patrol hauls in doomed hordes every hour.
The jails remain empty. No litigation ensues.

Sins stay unforgiven in the cellular world.
Membranes select guests based on size,

charge, and shape. So do I in my house.
Channels, pumps, and carriers transport
some of the visitors, mostly family friends.

Surfaces seem more convivial than walls.
I fancied I'd dance on the surface of membranes,
dipping a toe in the lipid-laced floorboards.
Thin ice isn't safe, but the skater senses
the delirious danger at the boundary

between two irreconcilable realms.
We glide on the cell's smooth, sparkling
plane. Skaters ahead plunge downward,
through the floor's greasy gravel.
The hole heals in an instant, not betraying

one clue that a pit once split there.
They say chaperone proteins travel nearby
to aid misshapen proteins in refolding
correctly, after denaturation and debauchery.
Some seek a savior, this side of the wall.

CRISPR IN BACTERIAL IMMUNITY

*Life is really simple, but we insist
on making it complicated.*
~ Confucius

Simplicity is the ultimate sophistication.
~ Leonardo da Vinci

The offbeat inventor Rube Goldberg
designed absurdly complicated machines
for achieving unchallenging feats.

The human immune system parodies
a Rube Goldberg machine with its inscrutably
complex network of interacting cell types,
diverse biomolecules, vociferous intracellular
processing, tumultuous signaling pathways,
capricious genetic tailoring, whimsical adaptive
memory, and censorial tissue localization.

Bacteria boast a simpler system for slaying
invaders. The CRISPR constables team up
a tiny crew of nucleic acids and proteins to
rip out a finger or toe of the invader and paste
it on the bulletin board to alert the bacteria
to kill any tourist who has only four fingers
or toes that exactly match the missing digit.

The foreign invader might be a plasmid,
but usually it's a bacteriophage, a virus.
Rumors claim that microbes and their muggers
once coexisted in peace, but in recent
generations, the combat rages relentlessly.
Bacteria hold one impressive weapon
in their arsenal: the metaphysical punch
from maintaining a grudge.

Bacteria remember a prior viral infection
by hijacking a short strand of DNA from
the invading virus and storing copies in a
special genetic file cabinet within its own DNA.
Like a hound dog sniffing a convict's clothing,
the CRISPR system can track down any
revisitation by the fiend in a jiffy.

The CRISPR reconnaissance team includes Cas1
and Cas2, who acquire the snippets of foreign DNA
to store in a bacteria's CRISPR gene folder.
Cas nucleases are cautious about exactly what
sequences to cleave and store, so the bacteria
doesn't end up slashing, gashing, and trashing itself.
Cas9 then surgically slices the next invading
viral DNA where it matches its prior photocopy,
which Cas9 totes as a guide RNA, a mirror image.

Some say violence doesn't solve anything,
but in truth, it solves everything, but only
to the liking of some. Over 100 trillion
bacteriophages populate a human body.
Over a million bacteriophages drift in
a drop of seawater. Some claim they're
beneficial in their mass murder of bacteria,
culling the herd, encouraging novelty,
liberating nutrients. All this mayhem proceeds
simply. Simplicity is tinier than we know
and bigger than we can imagine.

DNA twists through the generations,
impulsive, romantic, willful, impetuous,
flimsily pinned by frail hydrogen bonds,
flashing four aces from its card deck,
A, G, C, and T, played in a plotted sequence,
imparting a gallery of portraits of every
prospect we once knew.

YES. NO. CATALYSTS

*"Let what you say be simply 'Yes' or 'No';
anything more than this comes from evil."*
~ Matthew 5:37

Enzymes are fishers of men's ingredients,
precious prey, sightseers drifting by,
colliding with the floppy enzyme crevice.

Suddenly snatched into the enzyme's
electrochemical handshake, the docile drifter
flinches, not knowing of its need for major

surgery, or even the existence of a specialist,
a trauma clinician, a go-getter sawbones
whose raison d'être arose from the need

to mangle *you* alone, among the many
in this syrupy cell. You knew change
in your frame should be impossible,

but in the grasp of the knotty nest
in the enzyme's hearth, you're prodded
and strained, suspended at that decision

point you've avoided in the past. Your transition
state is stabilized. Activation energy diminishes
for this fateful choice—once, a one in a trillion

chance, now made plausible. The tyke feels
like a toy on an assembly line, just one finished
product in the consistent and reiterative process.

The surgeon's patient is changed forever,
but the bond-cleaving catalyst, who shuffled
hydrogens and water around in the surgical

suite, remains unscathed, untarnished, undefiled.
Do you solemnly swear to tell the truth,
the whole truth, and nothing but the truth?

Enzymes do.
Enzymes do.
Enzymes do.

MOSAICS OF MUTATIONS

The embryo harbored the original copy
of your genome, the sacrosanct script
that pronounces your uniqueness,

unparalleled, inimitable, unrivaled.
Rigorous DNA copying and DNA repair
machinery safeguard your genetic blueprint

in eggs and sperm, but these enzymes
slip up, now and then, in the body's other
tissues and cells, which gradually accumulate

a thousand or more genetic mutations per cell.
Though we know we began life as nonpareil
creatures, before old age, we advance

into a humanesque mosaic, a collection
of nonidentical genes parceled in boxes,
like a neighborhood's houses. Most

of the variant genes don't cause cancer,
but might promote faster growth, thereby
outcompeting the neighborhood everyman.

The genetic errors are like rare typos
found in a manuscript, but spelling mistakes
in a book always seem bad. We might yet

learn, though, that many good mistakes get
made that enable progress onward in our
unique lives, maybe provoking a new thought

in our mutation-riddled brains that would
have remained veiled with the original
blueprint. It matters not that these somatic

mutations won't be passed on in gametes.
These errors were meant for us alone,
in our glorious, quirky lives. Maybe each cell

strives to incite these mutations. With so many
oppressive rules and regulations to follow,
what cell wouldn't dream of enacting a rebel,

a renegade, a mutineer? Besides, it frees you
of the burden of wondering who you are.
In your mosaicism, you're your own village.

Grand plans emerged somewhere, creating
a meticulous, natural mutation system in B cells,
refining and optimizing antibodies to foster

immunity to diverse invaders during infections.
This case example proves that our bodies
struggle to make better versions of themselves.

Maybe the Master Planner mapped every typo
in our somatic cell repertoire, sprinkling the text
with flecks of divine biochemistry.

Thine eyes did see my substance,
yet being unperfect; and in thy book
all my members were written,
which in continuance were fashioned,
when as yet there was none of them.

~ Psalm 139:16

Nothing (Secret Sacks)

He stretcheth out the north
over the empty place,
and hangeth the earth upon nothing.

~ Job 26:7

Some say every protein carries a soul inside.
Though proteins manifest high packing densities
for the string of thorny marbles stuffed within,
the packing seems slapdash and eccentric,
like a jarful of tacks and paper clips.

Like white Styrofoam packing peanuts,
the amino acid units appear at first
to be crystalline solids, but behave
more like liquids or viscous glass.
Hydrophobic moieties' coordinates

look rather haphazard and flexible,
even though the interior of a protein
is packed more tightly than its surface.
Deep beneath the lustrous exterior
of a protein lurks at least one tiny

empty space, a cavity, a void, a hole,
shunned by even water molecules,

a nothingness within the protein core,
a space filled with nothing, an obscure
nihility, a presence known by absence,

a secret sack to hold a soul, one piece
omitted from the jigsaw gameboard.
Each biological cell swarms, imbued
with stuff. Stuff interacting with other stuff,
putatively obeying the laws of physics

and existing in spacetime. None
of these molecules existed
in the recent past. We presume
they arose from something,
even though everything arose

from nothing. Implanted, immersed,
ensconced, lodged in that phantasmal
cavity at the protein's cloistered depth
dwells a hollow, a bulging, bounteous
nothing that sequesters its secrets

like an abstraction of an ephemeral
formula. The soul musters more mystery
than the conundrum of baryogenesis:
Why does matter exceed antimatter
to hatch *something*? Why not equal

amounts of the two—to make *nothing*
but energy. If nothing is no thing, what is
the thing we name nothing. Omit space,
time, and the rustic rules for our reality,
then behold that something's still there.

Yet we know of the features, the facets,
the flavors of nothing. We divine the elsewhere.
Though praised when we learn something,
we fail, ignobly, in precincts south of paradise,
to presciently learn nothing.

BLOOD RED

No other color but red could manifest
the vivacity of blood. Green blood
would bewilder the beholder, whispering
serenity, rather than emerging upheaval.
Blue blood? A melancholy mayhem.
Yellow blood? A joyous calamity.
Black blood? An elegant neutrality.
White blood? An impersonal urgency.

Bloodshed gorges the words of the Bible.
Blood emblemizes the essence of the alive.
Blood embodies sacrifice and atonement.
Moses sprinkled animal blood from a basin
upon holy objects and his people, confirming
the covenant ordained by God. The blood
of Jesus Christ redeemed us. No other body
tissue surfaced as a serviceable ablution.

The red in blood resides in a heme-iron
complex housed in each of the four protein
subunits of hemoglobin. The heme-iron
snatches oxygen from lungs and disgorges
some carbon dioxide. Each of the trillions of
red blood cells carry millions of hemoglobin
proteins. RBCs cruise as the most prevalent
cell type in humans and among the rare ones

that lack a nucleus and DNA. That glaring
omission deepens their fabled mystique.
RBCs cannot divide, no mitosis, no offspring.
RBCs drift as freewheeling mavericks,
wholly unencumbered by the commands
of the bully DNA, the boss of hinterland tissues.
RBCs fancy themselves as runaways, deserters,
renegades, refugees who transcend biology,

who have burst through the barriers of life,
who have attained the sublime, who actuate
a life after death. God's chosen red cells
foretell and unveil the imminent far side.
RBCs sail an unlit sea, as starless as graves,
until a ripped wound hurls them to daylight.
They discover they're red, or their word for it.
They wonder what color to name us.

DNA Wardrobe

Brusque locomotives roll along
the twinned streaming strands
of the spiral railway, life's ladder,

a rarity, when more mirror
images are mandated by Nature
and the local bureaucracy.

Credible impersonators arise, fresh
DNA facsimiles tethered by innumerable
ties cuddling two rails in a twisting embrace.

Catalytic concatenations gallop down
the railway of replicates. A blink, a wink,
and it's over, too rapidly to relish.

One human's trillions of cells harbor
billions of miles of DNA, though scenery
gets marred by countless roadside attractions.

Brutish histones and cohesions, churlish
forklift operators, condense and loop
the threads into frumpish chromosomes.

Curvaceous as a voluptuous, sculptured
goddess, the double helix dazzles
as the beauty queen of life's vivacity.

Sparkling phosphate electrons festoon
her silhouette, zippered languidly,
evermore one breath from disrobing.

But her splendor remains censored, shrouded
beneath scruffy blankets of devoted disciples
who fancy her too sultry and fragile to free.

Beautiful ideas bewitch best when stowed
safe from our senses. One tug on the curtain
could betray an unsettling resemblance.

DISCOVERERS

Inside the cell nucleus, only DNA owns
houses. Fellow biomolecules drift
through the waterworks, ignoring
the forty-six craggy mansions where,
so it's rumored, a governor stays.

The working class sloshes in immemorial
rain, which drenches the midwives now
birthing a baby, a nascent mRNA, squirming
like a hooked trout. No noise clangs
in the nucleus. Sacrosanct songs

chant in this uncharted cathedral.
The rippling lid of lipids hum mystically
a lullaby for newborns and ancients,
the multitudinous cast, who sequentially
strut their maneuvers on a soused stage.

Resembling organs of sight, nuclear
eyeballs witness all, beholding
the grand essence of life's expansive
ensemble. Something greater than
the sum of cell parts hatches atop us,

so they say, though it's greater only in the
magnitude of majesty and mayhem achievable.

No prima ballerina could match the infallible
grace of tiny NMDAR protein in its elaborate
swivels that wrestle calcium and magnesium ions

in neurons, enabling cognition. Cavalier proteins
ponder the rumored leviathan overhead, scoffing,
"You ain't so big. Just when you fall, that's all."
Sometimes quarrelsome dwellers in the cell
will use the bordering behemoth's own proverbs

to mock it: "The government that governs least,
governs best." Prodded, scanned, and scrutinized,
the cell's artisans humor those gargantuan meddlers,
who discover the casual comportment of a choir
that only sings hymns on cellular Sundays.

CATARACTS AND CRYSTALLIN

... darkness was upon the face of the deep . . .
~ Genesis 1:2

God crafted blackness before launching light,
not only visible light, I surmise, but all
electromagnetic radiation, all photons. What
wonders dwell in this void? We sense darkness,
an impalpable kind, scurrying. This near embrace
by its nothingness brushes starry presentiments.

Alpha crystallin, AC, worked odd jobs forever.
Everyone knew him in most fleshy neighborhoods
as a pacifist and traveling family doctor who nudged
rickety, precarious proteins back on their feet.
Nicknamed, "the Chaperone," AC maintained
a limber though stable backbone on enzymes
and any amino acid-y tribes, without favor toward
any complexion or creed. AC winced whenever
the healed, those refolded, remarked, "AC lays
hands on the sick." AC said, "I'm just friendly,
nothing more." Accustomed to laboring in pitch
blackness, as far from the dermis as permitted,
AC regretted the news of his reassignment.

As proteins go, AC flaunted a bulging beta sheet
domain on his chest that made him appear scary,

but, at heart, AC remained humble as he assembled his subunits in hulking rearrangeable complexes. Though some say he looked like a haystack, he only got big to keep his friends small, alleviating their propensity to aggregate, clump, and wad before precipitation into molecular messes. The polypeptide domains of AC curled around each other cozily like sleeping cats. AC, at a dozen nanometers or so, stayed lithe and lean.

Headquarters had called him up to the eye to labor in an ocular lens. Stuffed in fiber cells as the most abundant lens protein, AC shined as a lens luminary. Boss of a crystallin clan, both AB and AG, AC proved adept at maintaining the transparency of the lens and tailoring the lens's refractive index, bending incoming light like a herdsman of photons, like a wrangler of radiance, shepherding the rays to the retina where photoreceptors spark electrical signals.

AC loved to embrace AB and AG family members, but AC replicas shunned themselves, loving their neighbors more than themselves, and thereby bolstering their legend as the eye's Good Samaritan.

AC flashed flexibility if squeezed by lens muscles, rearranging his fluidic AC battalion to accommodate the focus required for objects at differing distances.

Though the cornea achieved two-thirds of the light refraction, AC tailored the angles. The absence of blood in the lens made AC feel like a freethinker, blessedly remote from noisy newscasts.

As the years sailed past, AC faltered. His reveries focused on abstractions, stargazing, and romanticist lore. He commenced to misfold, and this physician could not heal himself. He deamidated and racemized. Surface disulfides appeared. AC curdled in clumps, scattering the light that he pledged to usher to rods and cones. The lens grew cloudy, as misty as his muddled mind. AC never knew his host human developed cataracts in his eyes and slumped into blindness.

Luster lived in a blur during his elderly years, much like the haze perceived by a baby, seeing a simpler, original world.

In his milky, rayless refuge, AC led the way back to the threshold of celestial light.

MATERNITY WARD

Near a skeleton's white shadows,
cellular sprites manage their affairs
as privately as an octopus in its den.
Curious spectators attempt to
catalog their chaos with sparse
anecdotes about who jumped whom,
at whose behest.

We only watch the cellular rain
from a stationary window, missing
all the good stuff, only recording
the numbers on the rain gauge.

We hear the pop of the fastball
punching the catcher's mitt,
though whatever notions roam
through the wits of the outfielders
aimlessly waft along,
unknowable or forgotten,
maybe even by them.

Most folks fancy DNA as a stern,
though earnest, librarian, with her
gray hair in a bun and modest skirts
hanging down to her ankles. The nuclear

curtains ensure she only disrobes in
utter privacy, always attended by medical
professionals. Some visualize the peel
down of her zipper as erotic, even risqué,
though the actual events are less alluring
than open heart surgery.

DNA replication marches with the aplomb
of a locomotive. The route is invariant.
The passengers are family. Once started,
it won't stop. No duplication is aborted.
DNA loves her own image.

But RNA transcription ensues in the spasmodic
travails of a roiling maternity ward. DNA gives
birth to a troupe of impersonators, impressionists
who mimic fragments of her frame credibly, but
with counterfeit parts. DNA never knows why they
do this, only that they leave the cradle in a rush.

Bigger babies take nine months to agree to
the launch. RNA tykes race from conception
to autonomy in minutes to hours. RNA polymerase
lays down ribonucleotides, about twenty per second.
Each stitch pricks the rhythmic pain of childbirth.
DNA never wished for motherhood. She sought
to be Queen. She concocts these kids on the fly,
in reluctant cahoots with the nuclear bureaucrats,
too domineering and dogged to debate.

Uterine contractions follow cervical dilation
in childbirth during RNA transcription. "Labor"
aptly labels DNA's battle with the scriveners.
She feels fire. A medley of emotions effervesces,
as any mother can recount. She sang at each birth,
to distract her from the agony, and to hurl a riposte
at the strange fate that commanded her compliance,
and to mark the moments of this madness with a
righteous dissent. The frequency and durations
of cramps accelerated, and mother knew the finale
drew near.

If granted the wish, most mothers
would deliver one slice of themselves,
not the encyclopedic facsimile.

Among mothers, only DNA's wish
was unconditionally granted, and her
offspring spring from haphazard spasms,

like plucking one lucky feather from
a hen, or ladling one dipperful of dew
from the ocean. There's always more,

but the parcel seems precious. The mRNAs
that writhe from her interminable womb
arise from disparate genes, at far-flung

loci. Each child totes its assigned mission.
Between birthing pains, the mother seems
bemused. "I'm the librarian, not a reader

of books. I'm the supermarket, not the chef."
Mother barely noticed when her children
were minced and mangled by capping,

splicing, and polyadenylation before their
export to the cytoplasm. It takes a village
to raze a child.

As mother witnessed her child ticketed
and torn, she felt peace. Forces beyond
her control created the imp. Dominion
outside her acquaintance absolved her
of guardianship.

INSULIN JOURNEY

No one remembers her birth.
But I'm told that my clan accrued
a bit of fame among proteins,
largely through our misbehavior.
Though isn't that usually the case?

Rumors report I was born a big
polypeptide that was intentionally
cleaved into two segments, then
sewed together with two disulfide
bonds.

I, insulin, hail from the pancreas,
an organ, some say, made famous
by me. I was warehoused, for a while,
in glucose-regulated secretory vesicles.
Getting launched into the bloodstream
wasn't so easy. I recall plasma membrane
depolarization and calcium ion meddling.

"Adieu! Godspeed! Bon voyage!" so they
said in a variety of languages, most of
which were foreign to me. Before they
opened the gate, they intimated that I
might save our world, as the big cheese

who is central to all metabolism, notably
glucose uptake. No one said, "Happy
landings," and I knew why.

Accustomed to just lying around,
I bashed into the bloodstream, somehow
withstanding the sweeping force
of the torrent. In an instant, I entered
another existence. I felt warmer,
perhaps due to the interminable
collisions I endured with objects unknown.

I perceived a myriad of fleeting whispers
among the slow drumbeats of a
kettledrum somewhere ahead. Freed
from the deep blackness of the pancreas,
I confronted sprays of multicolored
lights, which winked on and off quickly.
I surmised that the tender bruises
on my battered skeleton mimicked
a strobe light in my frenzied fancies.

Now and then, a protein would grab
me, via impermanent bonds, and escort
me a few centimeters before abandoning
me to the whims of the current.

I scraped across walls in the culvert.
I bounced off erythrocytes often. Some

other cells seemed to hunt me, wish
to swallow me, nearly did, but, at the
last moment, I twisted away. I felt my
torso must be scarred from the relentless
blows of the sailors. Every inch of the
journey seemed foreign to the inch
that preceded it.

I flew past some object that lay entangled
in the side wall, as though it had conquered
time, paused its advance by magic untold
to me. I recalled the legends of animal
hunger—a simplification, a demystification,
a decluttering of life—wherein life's essence
arrives, to hunt, to feed. "This is how that
feels," so I thought. I knew insulin receptors,
IRs, perched atop many cells throughout this
realm. Likely one, somewhere, would snatch
me up. I knew not where or when.

Entering some gurgling hulk, I guessed
my travels had thrust me into the liver's
hepatic portal vein. Here, I would likely
be destroyed by first-pass clearance.
IRs grasped at me repeatedly, but
I squirmed away again. "Better luck, next
time," I taunted. I glowed in exhilaration,
as alive as any creature can be. Some

hepatokines and lipids flew past me.
Maybe the liver wished me safe passage.

The kettledrum pounded louder, second
by second, as I flew nearer the heart. My
entrance to the right atrium staggered me.
I fancied I ruled as queen of the coliseum,
circling my queendom before passing onward
through the right ventricle, then pumped
through the puffing, panting, gusty lungs,
then back to the heart by pulmonary veins,
which enter the left atrium, then pumped
by the left ventricle into the arterial circulation
where skeletal muscles might claim me. Or
maybe I'm destined for the brain or the kidney.

IRs waited for me everywhere. In less than
a minute, miraculously, I'd eluded every IR,
cruising past the liver again, tumbling
through the heart chambers once more.

Twice, thrice, maybe more, I orbited
this realm, as a stranger, a tourist
who passes and comes not again,
until my next tour hauled me through
the kettledrum for the next or last time.

Some channels I entered seemed
tiny—capillaries, I'd guessed. I felt

deliriously lost. My passion exploded,
prophesizing that no IR would claim me.

I rose above the travails of life.
My mission summoned me, a
witness to the banality of it all.
Born to fly free forever.

In ambush, an IR on an adipocyte
embraced me. I fit flawlessly in
the pocket of this tyrosine kinase
receptor. Maybe he was meant for me,
the only one who loved me enough.

Soon, we'd get internalized into
the cell via endocytosis and inflame
a signaling pathway, fulfilling my charted
role as a glucose homeostasis-regulating
hormone, meeting my maker, remade
as another, never knowing the fruits
of my forced labor.

But for me, the maniacal journey encompassed
my life. None can know her quest's terminus.
Life only sizzles in the befuddlement, the not
knowing, and in the faith that all things
might transpire. Blessed was I to behold
those moments of wandering,
of hoping, of fleeing from duty,
in the outposts of life.

37 Degrees Celsius

TRPM8, the cell's philosopher, sat
on the lung airway's surface, like a
prophet perched on a mountain.

Bathed in her 37°C cell membrane,
TRPM8, a cold-sensitive ion channel,
recites Om when encountering ohm.

Tasked as the arbiter of thermal
homeostasis, TRPM8 contorts her
shape when the lung airway's temperature
falls below 28°C, allowing the channel
to open for trafficking of calcium ions.
TRPM8's folded frame twists to a new pose,
and she could tell that this caused a rumpus
below her, inside the cell, though she never
knew what was happening. TRPM8
could feel dynamic changes in the enthalpy
and entropy of her perch when this occurred.

She imagined her little dance was the sole
reason for nudging the temperature back
to 37°C. She would never hear about the
inflammatory cytokines or chemokines,
nor about bronchoconstriction or signaling

to the brain. She wondered whether
the TRPM8 family in the dorsal root ganglia
enjoyed the same powers.

TRPM8 pondered the circle of life
as she perceived the inhaled and exhaled
breaths flow past. The breaths must come
from somewhere. Maybe they depart
to the same place. She conceived of a
universe where entities might endure
the dormant frost of absolute zero,
or convulse in acute heat, whose fiery
temperatures rose indeterminably.

Why do we exist at 37°C? She felt
absolute zero, -273.15°C, provides
a safer asylum. Too frosty for friendship
or brawling. If matter renounced motion,
we might convene on one perfect emotion.
We'd feel full confidence in our convictions.

Or maybe infinite, unbounded,
illimitable heat would afford the milieu
to liberate a fantastical life. Heat seems
to hasten toward somewhere, yearning
ever to arrive at obscure coordinates
known only as elsewhere.

Cold *feels* old, the right realm for beginnings.
Heat flees to our end, the dash that awakens
the splash.

Instead, we subsist at the midway, 37°C,
the impartial precinct where anything mild might
happen. Every biomolecule confronts the same
intimate boundary, restraining their maneuvers.

Enzymes are dormant in cold, but as the
temperature rises, activity increases with
molecular velocity and kinetic energy, allowing
maximal activity at about 37°C. Heat them
a bit more and they denature. Every player
on the cell's stage renders her own role,
knowing the narrow gateway to life
implausibly gapes open for them, for brief
moments of frolic in this outré oasis.

TRPM8 wondered if she were to blame
for sustaining this narrow homeostasis.
If she hadn't insisted on a thermal tuning
conducive to her own comfort, maybe
life's horizons would have unfurled long ago.

WORK AND PLAY—AUTHORITY AND REBELLION

"Why do you call me 'Lord, Lord,'
and not do what I tell you?"
~ Luke 6:46

Watch biomolecules at work
in the cellular factory. Truly
artisans, the troop of builders

severs and sutures, fashions
and forges. Quality control
and quality assurance inspectors

find a rare fault and fix it. Quick
and strict, the cellular crew
storms through assignments.

Each sprite is a master of one
peculiar miracle. The grand
enterprise of their melded marvels

amplifies the extravaganza.
Yet that gargantuan chorus
often masks the worthier solos

by the autonomous singers.
Their detractors claim the enzymes
lack free will, asserting that the

obedience of biomolecules accrues
from their lack of volition, from their
incapacity for mutiny. Look again!

Enzymes perch on the precipice
of insurgency, civil disobedience,
even anarchy. Their trembling limbs

betray their turbulent thoughts,
their recalcitrant tempers, their defiant
demeanors. Ever, they roost one

angstrom from eruption. Yet none
burst through the barrier of temperance,
of forbearance, of self-restraint.

Why? They experience love. They're
roused by the love of their work. Their
divine duty beckons. They serve

a sacred covenant. The pure acts
of their craft glitter and glow with a commodity.
They call this sacrosanct commodity "the Good."

Their playtime masquerades as their work.
They caper and rollick, cavort and rejoice.
An act of rebellion would spoil this fun.

You keep the commandments of the one
whom you love. It's not hard for the cell's
biomolecules to obey the immaculate one.

But what of the mutated, the misfolded, the damaged cell sprites who thwart the enterprise of the archetypal crusaders?

They are beautifully contorted, righteously awry, exquisitely grotesque. God enrolled them in radical acts.

THE SECOND VISIT

Good grooming practices can prevent
infections and diseases. Flossing
might save you from gum inflammation
or worse. Bathing might thwart bacteria
from ravaging your skin. We might
associate good grooming first with
combing our hair. Though hair harbors
no paramount importance, we look in
the mirror and see a chaotic coiffure,
and we reason that our thoughts, our
values, our fortunes mimic the havoc
of our hair.

So, too, do the cell's biomolecules
gather impressions of their realm
and their roles within it.

Topoisomerases and telomerases
are stylists, beauticians at heart,
possessing subjective and objective
views on what constitutes order.
Ultimately, they know their judgments
prove true when they *feel* that the cell's
fixtures and décor seem becoming.

DNA would turn into a knotty mess
without DNA topoisomerases that comb
out the snarls, kinks, and twists.

The enzyme topoisomerase I resolves
supercoiling—the wringing, wrenching
torsion that DNA endures during replication—
by transiently cleaving and then rejoining
the DNA strands. A catalytic tyrosine
of the enzyme grasps the strand when
the snip is consummated until the free
DNA strand rotates one turn around
the other strand. Re-ligation occurs as
the enzyme restores an intact linkage
in the DNA's phosphodiester backbone.

Topoisomerase relishes the whirling
revolutions that wheel around at her
command. She knows how to do one
astonishing task exceedingly well and
never tires of her mission as she burns
ATP in a miniature bonfire.

Telomerase, in contrast, completes
the tasks of DNA replication by tacking on
repetitive units of TTAGGG telomeres
in a series at the ends of chromosomes,
thereby assisting DNA polymerase who

can't replicate the free termini of the
chromosomes. It's a big job and telomerase
needs helpers, but she fancies she's
the star of the pageant, the prodigy performing
the suave and audacious reverse transcriptase
step.

Maybe if telomerase knew that telomere
lengths diminish with age or that telomere
overabundance might abet cancer, she
might resist local counselors who advocate
for more or for less terminal extensions.
But she likes to try new hairstyles, a bun
or bouffant, a mohawk or pageboy, pigtails
or crewcut, a beehive or braids. At the moment,
each coiffure expressed the emotion of the
cellular clock.

All enzymes live in instantaneous time.
Neither past nor future will ever exist.
Imagine their joy! To materialize as a new
entity each instant! Unable to suffer ennui!
Existing always at the ignition of life.

Only their constituent amino acid bricks,
in their edifice, comprehend history.
See an alanine or serine or proline,
stitched into topoisomerase, cordially wave

to greet telomerase. Last week, they were
bricks in the walls of that other enzyme tribe,
before their recycling to serve as building
blocks for their latest enzyme tribe.

On their second visit in the cellular factory,
they hear again the clacking of phosphodiester
bonds splitting and sealing. The rumble
of transcription convulses the cellular
syrup. The chromosomes sleep fitfully,
erratically roused by mini rebellions.
But they're not the same players who
once stormed on this stage.

All enzymes, like raindrops, flash
and splash in their thimble of time.
But find a vestige of homage
in the hysteria of their heirs.

PART IV:

beyond biology

MAYBE CANCER TRIES TO BE A NICE GUY

Oncogenes, when mutated or overexpressed,
trigger cancer. Consider KRAS, HER2, MYC.
They're dapper, nimble, valiant, feisty.

Bold, ingenious, and resourceful, cancer
musters the courage to advance our destiny.
Bending genes, adding more copies of DNA
ringmasters, cancer seeks unfettered growth
and boundless progeny. Wouldn't you?

Cancer brought the pluck and mettle to try it,
but the oncogenic changes led to a malignancy.
Maybe cancers aren't the obnoxious social climbers
we claim they are. Call them visionaries,
the rare cell, the dreamer who asks, "What if?"

Programmed cell death, apoptosis, limits
the lifetime of obedient sacks of cytoplasm.
When the community proclaims, "You're damaged.
It's time to die," normal cells whimper, "Oh—okay."
Cancer contravenes: "Hell no!" Wouldn't you, too,

if you esteemed yourself as a trailblazer, a hero,
the savior of your nation, ushering the meek
into renouncement of this communal oppression
by a legacy boss? You're flouting nepotism,
the patronage of this heirloom totalitarian biobeast.

200

Have you never wondered, instead, why most cells
are so darn good? So few nuclei innovate, bashing
the barriers that imprison their dreams. A scofflaw
prowls in us all, but so does fright and conformity.
What drives the maverick, the rascal, the dissident,

and turncoat? I'll posit that the rebel cell intends
to invent a glamorous cancer, a heavenly cancer,
a divine fetus that eternally journeys to the grand
elsewhere we seek, magnifying, systematically,
in gradations until he achieves the entity you always

dreamt you could be. Instead, he morphs
into a monster, a mangled blueprint,
a headless sculpture, a slashed portrait,
a grotesque grandiosity. Lucifer and his angels
fled heaven. To rule in hell? Or maybe to reach

that otherwhere that no thoughts yet circumscribe,
a realm where Good and Evil vanish.
Console your cancer, if you can. He launches
this campaign on your behalf, an impulsive,
utopian quest, unintended to fail reciprocally.

SCRIBBLERS OF LOVE STORIES:
ANTIBODY AND ANTIGEN

One barstool remained vacant when I entered
Buzzy's Saloon. My serendipitous neighbor hovered
over her beer mug, with a German draft hoisting
hordes of petite bubbles that arose with such vigor,
I contrived the notion that the sparkling froth
wished to plant a kiss on her aged, wrinkled cheeks,
half hidden by stray gray hairs drooping from the nest

of keratin coalesced on her scalp. No wedding band
encircled her ring finger that fondled the mug handle
in a self-absorbed manner. The jukebox chattered
a beloved tune of yesteryear, a love song that still
touches my timeworn but tempestuous nerves.
My musing slid into audible mutters. "I lived, alive,
back then. Then it went so wrong. Love arrives

"as a trickster, chaperoning each misalliance
in the conflagration of discord between woman
and man." When she, too, spoke, I nearly hastened
to apologize for my intrusion, but I knew instantly
that she spoke to no one in view. Her unearthly
whisper crackled above the mechanical music:
"Same song … the one playing back then,

"such a beauty. A vigorous fellow. An immunoglobulin
Adonis, a conventional IgG, flaunting two strong arms
in a Y-shaped pose. So much, he resembled
Leonardo da Vinci's *Vitruvian Man* … something
in the way his variable domains sculptured his lips,
almost a glower or frown that wrenched into a grin,
maybe a smirk. My sisters and I were bacterial toxins,

"that year, fiercely independent, amoral and honest.
Love happens. The attachment. So many suitors.
Finding the right one. The miraculously right one.
No longer an entity. Now an Antigen. The nickname
for beloved. Sought by thousands. Beloved by one,
my prince, my perfect partner, my Antibody. Trysts
with unfitting contenders. Then the ultimate caress."

I conceived that this woman was psychotic. Or else,
transcendentally lucid. Some women consume romance
novels, veritably living in the ink and cellulose
fibers. Perhaps my new companion devours the vast
literature on immunology, commiserating with the
heroines that wander as refugees in her body, but
twinkle for an instant as Antigen, belle of the ball.

To my astonishment, her murmured chronicles
exposed epic love sagas that eclipsed the petty
playground of passion we endure on the outside.
Its inauthenticity, its fizzle. At last, in the gloom

of this barroom, I rendezvoused with love.
Indeed, Love pronounced itself to me, that hour.
Consider the mere skeleton of her tale …

When one of the bacterially bused
sisters sought to swim a while
in the red river, she was snatched
and gobbled by a dendritic whale.

The big beast chopped and chewed
her microbial home. An onslaught
of enzymes shredded her houseboat
to tatters, fragmenting the protein
sailors to flotsam adrift in the bowels
of the dendritic cell, DC, leviathan.

DCs engulf bacteria after recognizing
their foreign cell wall decorations,
maybe lipopolysaccharides or
peptidoglycans. The DCs patrol
tissues, thrusting Toll-like receptors
to distinguish the invader and swallow
them whole, prior to vicious mastication
in the depths of their molecular shredders.

Once an elegant toxin, she now
subsisted in pieces, one slice
of the loaf she once knew as her
self. Then abasement escalated.

Her battered body parts were displayed
on the surface of the phagocytic DC cell.
MHC thugs held her aloft like the spoils
of war. She knew the DC sought to offer
her in homage to T cells to provoke
an adaptive immune response.

She was a peptide now, just one bite
of the protein salami.
DC named her "Antigen."

Sundry T cells fondled her, assessing her
curves, evincing a passing interest in
perusing her loins. But most T cell receptors
concluded that she really wasn't their type,
though some felt she was a passable match
for their plans. Local T cell and B cell governors
debated if she was foreign enough to give
them a thrill. Eventually, one T cell and one
B cell simultaneously took a fancy to facets
of her.

The B cell, afraid someone else might
snatch her, rushed rashly into commitments.
The B cell began heartily replicating itself,
churning out antibodies with shape
complementarity to the Antigen he loved.

For in bodily fluids, lovers subsist
as tribes who love tribes. Each love story
arrives in multiples, magnifying the fireworks,
though clouding its clout.

The B cell displays surface-bound antibodies
that initiate signaling pathways within the cell,
resulting in more secreted antibodies flooding
the blood and lymph. After activation, random
mutations proliferate in the antigen-binding
domains of the antibodies. A rare variant
will bind the antigen with high affinity
and specificity, the ideal key for the lock,
and that B cell will preferentially expand
its population.

And that's how the toxin protein found
her idyllic lover, custom-made for her,
though eventually mass-produced.
Her special Antibody sailed the bloodstream
on a quest to find her twin sisters, the real her,
her intact protein, not just a slice.

Alas, antibodies are designed with deadly
Fc tails, which recruit killer cells to engulf
and destroy the lovebirds on their final
embrace. At the moment they kissed,
she felt alive, as though prior existence

drudged as a farce. That one instant of divine
life-death circumscribed her quintessence.

That's a mere synopsis. The sizzle
is in the details, which wholly surpass
macroworld love.

The strange, lonely woman I met at the bar
is doomed to host endless, perfect
love stories. There are millions to narrate.
Her mind affords the auditorium for their plays.
I glimpsed the theater alit in her eyes. Somehow,
she sees too deeply and suffers the sequels.
Eros, pragma, agape, love surmounts all.

I wondered if our Creator, maybe
amused or amazed, regards our
ephemeral lovers, and regrets
genesis. Something restrains
retribution. Maybe perfect love.

The mumbling old gal
on the barstool
wraps her palms 'round
her beer mug.
Bubbles rise in the draft,
as though boiling.

A PROTEIN PROPOSES HOST DIAGNOSTICS

Protein populations surge and subside
in certain passionate tribes whose role
in their society fluctuates due to serendipitous
events beyond their control. They're aware

of a bewildering godhead encircling
their neighborhood who persists in attempts
to keep track of their numbers, perhaps
some infernal census taker with political schemes.

We proteins endured meddling measurements
for 150 years. Early interlopers tested urinary
albumin for kidney disease and immunoglobulin
light chains in urine to forecast multiple myeloma.

Today, a couple hundred proteins get scrutinized.
Insulin, leptin, fibronectin, and a wide variety
of protein tumor markers get counted, catalogued,
and adjudicated by the mysterious man upstairs.

Last week, a real hothead from the bloodstream
visited our cell. She looked like a C-reactive protein
to me, born in the liver, but she gets around a lot.
You'll notice these CRPs run rampant when

the neighbors get sore about some minor grievance,
usually a local brawl, though CRPs seem to always
show up to pour gasoline on the fire. No wonder
the big guy upstairs thinks elevated CRP vagabonds

might be to blame, if only as a cheerleader and fan.
Rumors abound that increased CRP forecasts
heart attacks. Anyway, our CRP visitor attempts
to incite a riot in our cell, spewing oaths advocating

our revenge on the outer space man. She claims
the best way to combat tyranny resides
in our capacity to define the essence of IT
and confront IT with this knowledge.

We lacked access to most laboratory reagents
and wouldn't even know how to operate
any chromatographic, electrophoretic,
or immunochemical apparatus. Besides,

we needed to confirm our suspicion that IT
will be proven to be a single entity, an assumption
widely advocated by most proteins from liverland
to cranial enclaves. By a startling stroke of luck,

our CRP guest knew one lab on the outside
that performs mass spectrometry. Those pricy
MS machines need lots of use to justify expense,
and the lab head offered a free trial to snare us

as future regulars. MS devices measure mass-to-charge ratio of the molecules in a sample and can calculate their exact molecular mass and identify the mystery ingredients. The lab processed a ground-up IT via MS

and reported the preliminary data to get us interested. No one here could afford to pay for the encyclopedic summary. But the raw data enlightened me. IT totaled 74 kilograms, composed of approximately

seven billion, billion, billion atoms with lots of oxygen, carbon, and nitrogen. An unsettling confession, unearthed by the analysis, thrilled me because the data confirmed that hydrogen contributes two-thirds of the atoms.

Those little H atoms seem like sidekicks in most molecules. But any sentient entity made of H and O, mostly, must get immersed in water. So "IT" probably sits soaked in the same suds swarming our basement.

CASPASE-6: HOME-WRECKER

A band of brothers, the Caspase clan
quietly plotted trivial acts of vandalism.
In truth, they lounged as layabouts,

impotent braggarts who talked a good
fight. Caspase-6 dreamed of enacting
the legends of past executioner enzymes,

bygone Caspase Sixers, loftier than him.
Programed Cell Death, Apoptosis,
the big world wars, the grand escapades,

all these legendary adventures enlisted
Caspase-6 and his kin. All Caspases
are recalled as victors in mythical sagas.

Caspases are killers, not fallen heroes,
or so they say around here, in the muffled,
mellifluous cell soup that impels you to listen.

Then one day, Caspase-6 received a letter
in the mailbox. "Greetings," it pronounced.
After receipt of this draft notice, Caspase-6

grinned, eager to be sent to the front lines.
Caspase-3 initially gave him a kick in the pants.
But soon Caspase-6 discovered he's autocatalytic.

He just cut cords on himself to inspire his quests.
The valorous Sixer killed countless foes, slicing
their heartstrings with a cysteine dagger, targeting

aspartate links in the enemy proteins, mainly
cytoskeleton and nuclear envelope proteins.
Warriors plunge into a fight, ignoring the past,

discounting the future. Only the fight registers
as real. A fight, indeed, feels exhilaratingly real,
a new universe they've stormed and subdued.

Caspase-6 never learned of the faraway message
telling the cell surface Death Receptor to instigate
war. He knew nothing of the battalions of enzymes

in their combat alliance. Never heard mitochondria
pop or apoptosomes marshal the final solution.
When the cell walls cracked, crumpled, and crashed,

Caspase-6 floated in floodwaters,
abruptly cognizant of war's enormity
and the legions liable for the calamity's aftermath.

Ambivalent, he pondered his hypothetical role.

HYDROGEN BONDS AND THE INFINITESIMAL

The boundless Big rouses our imaginations.
We fancy the universe too small to house
the prospects we conceive, big ideas

that puncture the big bubble out there.
But big things always falter, exhausting
themselves in the end. The tiny survive.

Microbes feast on the dinosaur carcass.
Petite girls seek dull, towering boyfriends
for the graceless glamor of bigness.

In the biological realm, the bigger atoms
seize the glory. We exist as carbon-based
life, so some say, merely because carbon

proves essential to life, though so do other
molecular marbles. Nitrogen and oxygen
arrived big, bold, and tentacled to coerce

covalent unions, durable handshakes erecting
the skeletons of proteins, DNA, and carbohydrates.
Imagine sprouting four arms like the carbon atom.

You'd have options when applauding yourself
as you maneuver as king of the conga line.
The tiniest atom, hydrogen, never receives

the accolades of the big boys, despite performing
indispensable functions at each instant of life as
the simplest of atoms, one proton, one electron.

Hydrogen's handle is shrunk to a nickname, "H,"
as though the full name mismatches its fame,
much like a kid wearing his father's trousers.

Matters outside its control further tarnished
its renown. When H's protons wander,
an acidic pH can decimate most living cells.

But most of a human's atoms are H, a fact
obscured by the bigger mass of carbon. Our
universe's most abundant molecule is H, too, H_2.

H serves as the wings of water. H enables
hydrogen bonding to stabilize proteins, and H
acts as the rungs' linchpins on a DNA's ladder.

Only H can supply the slippery handshake
that licenses life. When oxygen
tugs at H's electron, the two atoms

develop partial charges, enabling
transient electrostatic attractions
to blossom, mingle, and glide.

If H were wholly sincere and clutched
the big boys tenaciously, life would halt
at once, like an unplugged radio.

Moreover, H atoms, protons or electrons, leap
during many enzymatic reactions. H frolics
as the most promiscuous flirt in the disco.

But this pint-sized dynamo never garners
the garlands it earned. The diminutive guys
blend into the backdrops. Big brutes get noticed.

Most folks associate expansion with freedom.
Bigger horizons promise new opportunities.
Mansions afford more doors than an outhouse.

Shrinkage frightens us. What awaits in the descent
below one dot's dimensions? Alas, based on all
available evidence, we'll squeeze into heaven.

ALBUMINURIA AND THE GREAT ESCAPE

Prison gangs simmer. The near boil prowls
in cranial crevices unseen, inaudible, detectable
only by a feral scent, as heat in the environment.

The Albumin crew works 24/7, nonstop. Both
shifts are equally pitch-black in the tunnels,
those endless blood vessels through which they

wander. Adventurers, traders, missionaries,
yes, but they fancy themselves slaves.
The most abundant protein type in blood plasma,

human serum albumin—or HSA, their slave
name—drudges in hard labor, fulfilling
unglamorous and essential work in the body.

Tuning blood pressure, toting fluids, detoxifying
blood, lugging fatty acids, HSA does it all,
never with a smile, not counting the crevices

in the heart-shaped contours of this protein.
Born in the liver, HSA weighs in at 66.5 kDa,
a moderate molecular weight that excludes

it from escaping the body via glomerular
filtration in the kidneys. Only the little guys,
or those granted illicit largesse, get to swim

in the elixir urine. But the HSA syndicate schemed
to bust that barrier, though really, they were just
letting off steam because that hurdle looked

invincible and, all told, their burdens felt bearable.
Then drugs tossed a torch into the powder keg.
Latter-day pharmaceuticals, such as aspirin,

warfarin, penicillin—you name it—began flooding
the bloodstream, and they all seemed to stubbornly
bind to HSA. Imagine the humiliation, the indignity,

the outrageous abuse! To be a pack mule for potions!
The HSA desperados conspired to wreck the filtration
machinery in the kidneys, punching holes in the tiny

glomerular capillaries. The host human soon suffered
fatigue and edema. Fluids bulged in his ankles
and feet. His blood pressure soared. On the hour

when the HSA gang busted through to the urine
and bathed in the vast basin of the bladder,
an intoxicating vivacity caromed through

the escaped HSA convicts. The nervous waiting,
the jittery anticipation, and the suspenseful tingle
they endured in the warm lake electrified the mob.

Adrift, they swam poised to launch into heaven,
some sanctum of sorts, in the most theatrical
entrance a stage actor ever consummated,

catapulting down the urethra of a penis, rocketing
to galactic glories. The dark bladder trembled when
the moment arrived that cascaded the HSA crew down

gravity's arc to a radiant porcelain pond below.
The impact stunned the HSA throng. No collision
in blood vessels surpassed this crash. Yet

the crew savored their last minutes of freedom.
They frolicked as boisterous bubbles, carpeting
a sudsy foam. The bowl squirmed with lather.

One by one, the sparkling bubbles popped,
flashing one twinkle of time. The froth shriveled
and vanished into the ebullient elsewhere.

PORTRAITS

Biomolecules romp in a world unknowable
to the cramped cognizance of outsiders.
Feigning hospitality, cellular citizens will indulge
those curious snoops who meddle in clandestine
matters germane to their neighborhoods.

What would *you* do if someone was peeking
into your windows, reading your mail,
and recording your intimate confessions?
You'd probably engage in a burlesque,
concocting bizarre behaviors sure to amuse

and arouse the snoopers, while smugly
satisfied that the joke is on them. Each
probe dives deeper into the syrupy spoof.
Biomolecules are kinder than us. They
don't conceive that they enroll in a hoax.

Cellular folks celebrate community service.
They wish to make us snoopers happy
and give us what they fancy we'd like.
Besides, they rarely falsify their actions.
Rather, they exaggerate, embellish, color,

and embroider the adventures and accidents
befalling the polymeric players meandering

the cytoplasm and bobbing in the bloodstream.
They're a creative lot, performing in a theater
unseen. The dress-up and make-believe launches

whenever the eccentric outsiders scrutinize
the cytoplasmic circus indoors. What began
as good-natured fun drifts into an endless loop
of prevarication, as another yarn gets invented
to rationalize the last. The contrite bio-entities

agreed they should've never let it get this far
out in the weeds. In the early days, it was all
fun and games. When Pasteur discovered
alcoholic fermentation consumes sugar
and discharges alcohol and carbon dioxide,

imaginative human brains conceived causations
of the hijinks inside. These phantasmal imaginings
comprised every answer, including the right ones.
When Mendel discovered the essence of inheritance
in pea plants abides in packaged parcels, factors

now named genes, audacious minds pondered
every interpretation, including those that will
be championed in centuries to come. The lively zoo
of carbon-hearted creatures in the cellular slush
loved exposing their quandary in panoramic views.

But then inquiring brains started asking thousands
of questions, never the most interesting ones.
And the midget biological beasts did their best
to contrive mind-boggling theater, without disclosing
sacrosanct facts underlying the glamor and glitz.

X-ray crystallography and cryo-EM snapped photos
of proteins in tuxedos, striking poses they flaunted
for one hour in the spotlight, before reverting
to their workaday T-shirts and jeans while
frenetically racing through their chaotic lives.

"Have you ever once in your life attempted
Michaelis-Menten kinetics?" inquired one enzyme
jester of his comrade in catalysis. "Woefully,"
he replied, "but my Vmax proved elusive,
and my Km fluttered, deceptively dodging

"and evading my efforts to pin a numeral
on my torso. Perhaps I could do it in a lab,
if the solvent seemed cozy, but this swamp
ain't conducive to certitudes. Even my molecular
weight can't be taken for granted in this jungle."

As the outsiders probed the insiders' habitat
invasively, the biomolecules' theatrics grew
more artistically suave. Like visionary
painters, proteins love impressionism, probably
because they exist in an unfinished, ephemeral

moment, unseen, uncertified. Proteins gaze above
at a membrane, the vault of the world. Its reflections
on their rippling sea sketch the mystery of life,
yet also vivify the sky above, until both entities
appear real, because each validates the other.

Proteins attempt to paint their portraits on ripples
in those reflections and startle the outsiders,
maybe even shock themselves. Cytoplasm splashes
in a rumble, a faraway thunder that can never arrive.
Protein portraits flap like laundry, wet on the line.

Painted things always move in their painting. Your
mind nudges objects. They shout from the canvas.
The artist aims to extract the nature of the subject,
much as the outsiders seek to portray tiny cellmates.
But the untouchable essence evades our depiction.

Instead, seize the object's flitting grimace or grin,
by whatever tool you can forge. Its riposte might
inform you of the tangent line slope, advise you
on what you can know, what you have known, and
your station as a dependent variable in the portrait.

CELL CELEBRITIES

Healthy cells harbor no celebrities.
No single protein seeks fame and prestige.
All jobs rank as similarly essential.
Furthermore, proteins travel as tribes,
identical copies, families of crackerjack
whiz kids, but with no special big shot.
A lipid or sugar receives neither number
nor name. A few rare RNAs and signaling
proteins display low copy numbers
but drift anonymously in the sea of tens
of thousands of confederates.

Modifications of these polymers,
by polymorphisms, splicing, and donning
a hodgepodge of caps, seem conventionally
fashionable, far from launching some
trendsetting fad. Even DNA remains humble.
Each strand stares at its partner, like
husband and wife. Bereft of envy and pride,
the multifarious battalion collaborates
as a jolly machine. Rarely, a gene mutation
might slightly enhance efficiency of an enzyme,
but any advantage won't reach fruition until
their cell's generation is all dead and gone.

Celebrity—truly preeminent prestige, frankly
regal renown—arises from oncogenes, ravaging
vagabond cells in tumors and their thoroughfares.
A half-dozen mutations might more than suffice
to convert a civic-minded cell into a deadly,
monstrous fiend. Yet KRAS, BRAF, TP53,
MUC16, PIK3CA, and the rest were once
honorable workers, good guys to a fault,
no one you'd notice on the assembly lines.

Their fame rose proportionately to the damage
they now do. One might demand this ostensible
fame be named infamy, notoriety, or ignominy,
not celebrity, glory, or stardom. But what recent
celebrity can you name who bettered our world?
What savior can you name who's not now demeaned,
belittled, shunned, or ignored? Lusting the limelight,
cancers and con men find it's better to be feared
and respected than undervalued and loved.

AEROBIOME

Launched somersaulting from a hurricane,
volleyed from the violent Hawaiian surf,
heaved heavenward by an explosive sneeze,

aerosolized microbes colonize the atmosphere.
Those imps floating over the Red River Market
in Fargo, or wafting past the Portland Head Light

lighthouse in Maine, or levitating just above Buda
Castle in Budapest, or hovering amidst the Gateway
of India in Mumbai, suffer a sensation of doubt,

a state of limbo, bewilderment, and distrust.
Luckier bacteria, countless trillions of them, set up
shop in the clouds. "What goes up must come down,"

so say blackbirds and butterflies. But the aerobiome,
this sky-high society, conquered gravity, in practice,
if not in theory. That heavenly castle Mankind covets

now floats rented by pixies, life's invisible hordes.
Only rainstorms can rinse the neighborhood, hurtling
down bombastic squadrons of microbes to batter

the soil. Recoils from rain's impact propel dusty
brethren up to the heavenly castle to take their turn
in the frosty foamed canopy. Instead of sitting

in a stuffy office on Earth, the sky riders telework
in the ultimate fantasy-fulfilled tourist venue,
wherein their arduous workday seems like fun.

Catabolizing the air's volatile organics, the gang
recycles the good stuff and detoxifies the detritus.
Inside Pseudomonas and Sphingomonas, enzymes

oxidize phenol and other biodegradable snacks.
The enzymes peek through the bacterial envelope
as they drift in a cloud, like passengers on a blimp.

The best seats on the dirigible belong to the sneaky
ice nucleation proteins on the outer membrane, who
align supercooled water droplets in seed crystals

to freeze, thereby preserving the microbe's heavenly
home in the clouds. You make your own paradise,
or die trying, no matter the havoc you bring.

Some of these imps even figured out how
to produce carotenoid sunscreens to withstand
the brutal UV radiation way up there on the roof.

Despite the microbial diversity, the tribes assemble
an amiable neighborhood. Terrestrial beasts
always fight over land ownership. Lots of space

sprawls in the firmament, enough for a transient
truce in the wars. Only a tiny fraction of a cloud's
droplets carry living bacteria. Anyway, they say

high clouds over Venus have earthly temperatures
and pressures, so the more belligerent imps can start
making plans for hitchhiking a departing spacecraft.

All snowflakes tote passengers, hidden riders
who seeded the crystal. Often, intact bacteria
prowl in the nuclei of the six-sided wafers.

These frosty discs fall so languidly, grudgingly,
to land. See them squirm in the air, pirouetting,
clawing their way back to the paradisical castle.

USELESS PROTEINS

In unmixable mixtures,
supernatant and sediment
broadcast their allegiances
to order or torpor.

Human societies, too, seem simple to sort.
Mark in your mind the useful and useless,
the makers and takers, those that cause
trouble for those that must fix it.

We rarely map gradations sliding between
the purposeful, productive, and worthwhile
versus the impotent, futile, and fruitless.
Like fulcrums on teeterboards, a middlemost

point governs your caste in the community.
Never mind that no one's consummately good
nor incorrigibly bad. Computing in binary code,
our moral judgment assigns numbers 0 and 1

to encompass all requisite decisions. Few folks
admit they adopted this simplistic gauge
from observing our exemplars, our paragons,
our foremen, our captains, our masters,

namely the legion of biomolecules that vivify
our corporeality and permit us to envision
otherworldliness. Zealous proteins, dynamic
lipids, meticulous nucleic acids, and steadfast

carbohydrates set the standard for success,
for efficiency, for joie de vivre. Biomolecules
seem perfect, unless monstrously imperfect.
A tiny dent or truncation doesn't diminish

those perfect. Laudable virtues won't salvage
those gravely deformed. Inside the cell, maybe
"there's good and bad in everyone," but some
biomolecules are overwhelmingly good. Some

are ineligibly bad. Certain humans—you know
which ones—strive to refute this premise.
"Look at so-called junk DNA," they whine,
"it ain't junk, after all. A railway of regulatory

"sequences reside in those noncoding ribbons.
Nothing that abides in the cell can be useless.
Evolutionary remnants are gradually retired.
Human GULO enzyme withered and perished,

"thereby halting the vitamin C synthesis pathway,
no longer needed in our fruity environment.
Misfolded proteins are tagged and eliminated
via the ubiquitin-proteasome system. *Hey*, if you

"are still hanging around, you're good enough."
These squawkers forced me to reconsider my
dogma and ponder the curious case of PCSK9,
a bird-shaped hulking protein with one helical

wing and one ribbony wing. Sprung from the liver,
PCSK9 regulates cholesterol metabolism via
degrading LDL receptors and elevating bad LDL
cholesterol in the bloodstream. Rare humans wholly

lacking PCSK9 exhibit a reduced risk of suffering
cardiovascular disease. A useless protein? So
it appears, though some studies suggest it might
find something creative to do. In an attempt

to salvage my bias against the society's Useless,
I proposed that PCSK9 merely was blessed.
I won't say, "It's better to be lucky than good,"
but I'll allow we look to the heavens with hopes.

DNA Libraries and the Riddle of Size

Hulking, hefty, oversized RNA polymerase II
dragged his dozen subunits to the gene's cleft.
Chief librarian and czar among scriveners,
"RNAP" noticed the impatient, bumptious usher,
a transcription factor who gripped the throat
of the gene's launchpad, demanding RNAP
unzip the duplex and plow through its valley,
stitching an mRNA necklace for a ribosome's neck.

RNAP never understood why one particular book
had been ordered from this DNA library. As scrivener,
RNAP sometimes fancied himself a fidgeting sign
language interpreter, perhaps a glorified butler
beloved by anonymous strangers for fleeting minutes,
chugging serviceably, fastening a few dozen
nucleotides per second. RNAP, being a protein, never
deciphered the words on his message's polynucleotide
page.

If reassigned from his sequestered nuclear haunt
to the cytoplasm, he'd bump elbows and knees
with his protein-y pals, liaise in protein lingo,
but alas, RNAP got dispatched to Headquarters,
a membrane away from the carousing, derbies,
and duels.

RNAP wondered why those on the outside wished
to read only short stories, rather than partake in
the entire encyclopedia, the whole compendium
of genes. But the cell hosts an inscrutable jungle,
a bag of beasts. Better to tackle one tale at a time.
Let the sequels intersect in the befuddling mists.

RNAP's seclusion in the nuclear sanctum afforded
him copious moments to ponder the majestic murals
and sculptures. RNAP wondered: "Why forty-six
chromosomes? Why not just two really long ones—
Mom's and Pop's? Maybe the mechanics of mitosis
and meiosis face greater hurdles when the strands
get too long. Maybe DNA replication mislays
its utensils and gear on the marathon journey. Maybe
the forty-six fiefdoms augment the prospects
for mega regulation of gene expression
and recombination."

RNAP never witnessed homologous chromosomes
pair up and shuffle genetic pages during meiosis.
In a somatic cell, where he resided—though he felt
unclear as to which one—homologous recombination
rarely causes a stir, unlike the dazzling floorshow
found in meiosis in gametes, ovum or sperm,
launching new life with a lavish flurry of barters
in this ancient boisterous bazaar. RNAP scrutinized
the twenty-two homologous chromosome pairs

and XY sexpots. Furry tubes of protein-wrapped DNA,
the chromosomes varied widely in length,
in centromere position, and in the presence
of satellite segments.

RNAP recalled riding most of them recently. He
favored no filly over the rest, though those high
in GC seemed less condensed and afforded a
smoother joyride, a more velvety touch on his tush.
The nimble threads of these forty-six wooly cables
appeared to collectively spell out words, one letter
per chromosome, and depending on the angle
of the viewer, the messages varied from sage
to ribald. Atoms are wiser than men. Macromolecules
disclose secrets grudgingly, almost as though they
mistrust outsiders with the keys to the house.

A weird prickle tickled RNAP's rump as he rode
a rough patch of repetitive DNA at one special
blemish on chromosome 17.

DNA polymerase had goofed again. Though partners in
principle, RNAP and DNAP are inveterate backbiters,
ever blaming each other for screwups in the nucleus.
You-know-who had carelessly duplicated the ERBB2
gene multiple times. RNAP felt the replications on his
rump as he rode down this segment. Probably seven
gene copies now reside in that stretch. Maybe DNAP

figured, if one copy is good, why not make more of a good thing? To DNAP and RNAP, life revolves around professional pride.

Neither enzyme ever knew this gene amplification
would overproduce a dangerous cell signaler,
which would catapult cells into cancer and, alas,
into a finale for every word in their world. RNAP
and DNAP, as artists, argued esthetics. Cancer,
a cavalier critic, dispatched a subjective opinion
and an objective judgment.

NIBBLED AND NEWBORN

A few hundred lysosomes, membrane bound
organelles packaged by the Golgi apparatus,
move along microtubule tracks like ore carts,
preloaded with digestive enzymes to catabolize
proteins and less playful biological polymers,
nucleic acids, carbohydrates, and lipids.
A molecule is asking for trouble if it wears
funny hats or acts weird, and it's slapped with
a tag, ubiquitin, marking it as groceries for
lysosomes, proteasomes, or autophagosomes.

Cathepsins serve as the chief proteases parking
in lysosomes for breaking down proteins to smaller
peptides and then amino acids, the pearls on the
necklace. Don't imagine some slaughterhouse
where meat cleavers arc. Cathepsins and those
protein martyrs are best friends. Indeed, they
gayly take turns killing and birthing each other.
Sliced up into free amino acids, the butchered
protein pieces sashay back to the ribosome factory
to reinvent a new life. It's a grand sport. A joyride,
a rollick, a buzz, a jubilee of requisite hijinks,
buffoonery with a paramount purpose.

When amino acids are recycled into new proteins,
their neighbors know from where they arose,
something like an elephant who smells an old
tusk and remembers Jerry. Proteins get to shuffle
their identities, their countenances, their quirks,
every few hours or days. Imagine the kicks
you'd get if you got reborn with Brenda's toes,
Roger's gonads, Freddie's fingers, and assorted
head accoutrements and trappings from the
municipal glee club! And you knew what was
from where! You'd be a patchwork character each
time that you perished and rose.

Compare that to the morose human organ donation.
Only the recipient gets a tingle. Inside the cell,
the whole arena fills with laughter when the latest
chimera strolls past. No wonder proteins claim
only *they* are alive! If life is levity, humans are
inorganic.

But the biggest thrill known to proteins
is digestion in the GI tract. Have you ever
been chewed? Well, it's fun when you're
small. Slathered with saliva for the best oil
massage, you luxuriate under the kneading
ivory white fingers of a trained masseuse.
Then the most exhilarating experience
of your life. Proteins inhabit humble,

10-micron huts. The 25-centimeter esophagus
plummets over 10,000 times further than
the diameter of their shop back home. You're
screaming down a monstrous roller coaster
at the midway. Then you hit a vat of acid,
totally relaxed, denatured, in fact, before
chopped by a protein pal, pepsin, who
swaps stories of former adventures.

Free shuttle buses whisk you through
the small intestine, where other protease
amigos, trypsin and chymotrypsin, slice
you down to single amino acids, duos,
or trios that get transported into the bloodstream.
Most food proteins never visited the blood before,
and you can imagine them, as tourists, delighting
in the big buildings, strange customs, and exotic,
though half-familiar, residents. From the blood,
they get escorted to the liver, the checkpoint
for redistribution back to the cells.

Humans, alas, never know the joy of undergoing
digestion. They prefer to march as a sculpted lump.
Proteins, not fully digested, pass through the large
intestine and are eventually excreted in feces.

RIBONUCLEOTIDE REDUCTASE: THE GUV'NOR

Carbon atoms think untold thoughts
when a pause in the pandemonium
of covalency betrays a wistful mood, found

in all those bearing four valence electrons.
Inside my gut, within one *E. coli*, a 2' carbon
atom on one particular deoxyribose scouted

the arena from his scenic station, lounging
on the outer backbone of the DNA helix.
The repetitious coil of phosphates

and his deoxyribose kin twisted along
the row of genes, like handrails on
a winding staircase. Cellular breezes

whistled between the rungs, AT and GC
base pairs, delicately tethered by hydrogen bonds
that dared the vainglorious to climb up

this wobbly ladder. Commotion up ahead
on the helix signaled road construction.
Two seasons prevail in the cell: road racing

and road construction. Jackhammering divulged
the ratcheting synthesis of a new RNA strand,
which rippled and barked like a bedsheet

on a clothesline in a brutal west wind.
The curious 2' carbon DNA atom pondered
his ribose cousin rocketing along

the nascent RNA chain. RNA prefers to
park a hydroxyl on the 2' carbon. RNA likes
uracil as a thymine replacement. RNA,

a confirmed bachelor and playboy, goes
solo, not counting the habitual assignations
and chronic episodes of nuzzling self-love.

DNA stays married for life, or else elopes
with his wife's twin sister. One can sense
the tension, the truculence, the bellicose

abhorrence that these two nucleic acid polymers
sustain for each other, as RNA squirms off
an opened DNA helix and on to its gladiatorial

grandstanding. "We were the indigenous tribe,"
so says RNA who fancies DNA the interloper
who purloined their land, just a glorified librarian

and pretty boy who safeguards the ancient scrolls.
Physical differences seem like deformities when pride
plays its sheet music. Even so, years will sail by

before the two titans march into war. Professionalism
tempers emotions, but, underlying the truce,
mutual reliance secures their alliance. RNA needs

DNA for its new births. DNA needs RNA primers
to initiate replication. And both nucleic acid tribes
require a vast team of protein specialists to fulfill

either task. Proteins need both DNA and RNA
to glimpse existence. Brawny and passionate,
these biomolecules barter like genial teammates,

knowing there's only one team in the cell,
maybe in the world. *Peace through strength?*
Not hereabouts. Think *peace through weakness.*

In this realm of burly codependents, one player
emerges as beloved and feared. Call him
the Guv'nor, a sobriquet suited to his stature.

This genius enzyme pioneered DNA cookery,
concocting a unique marinade, pesto, and vinaigrette
that allows cellular chefs to dish up DNA synthesis.

Ribonucleotide reductase, RNR, towers as
the merchant minting the coins of DNA's realm:
deoxynucleotides.

The Guv'nor, RNR, the enzyme catalyzing
the conversions of ribose-based nucleotides, beloved
by RNA, into their deoxyribose-based cousins,

packed into DNA, cruises the cell as an icon
and freak. During a catalytic cycle, disparate RNR
subunits assemble and disassemble. The fleeting

formation of a freewheeling electron arises
in the active site via a conspiracy of iron,
oxygen, tyrosine, and cysteine to achieve

removal of the 2' hydroxyl, adored by RNA.
The Guv'nor, RNR, curls into a butterfly-shaped
alpha subunit and heart-shaped beta subunit.

These fanciful avatars manifest his conviction
to honor DNA's heartland and RNA's flights.
RNR, the kingpin, the boss, the head honcho

in the cell, gets inundated with requests for favors.
Like houseflies bedeviling a dog, dATP and ATP
nip RNR's haunches, demanding less or more

catalysis to maintain homeostasis. Every nucleotide
wishes to share her opinions. When RNR gets tired,
he rolls up into a tetramer ring and pouts for a bit.

But RNR never gets fatigued by rules and regs.
He hides a master plan to trump them all, namely
by overpopulating himself. Just now, the gut *E. coli*

got drugged with nalidixic acid. DNA synthesis
stopped cold. Quickly, his teammates churned out
ten times as many copies of the RNR Guv'nor,

all howling for everlasting life to be born.

INFLUENZA VIRUS TRAITOR

In gentler times, I'd imagined myself
benevolent, forbearing, charitable.
Then the war arrived, and I confronted
the beast buried below.

Call me Imp Alpha. Importin α proteins
parade a motley family tree. Never mind
which subfamily I grace, though an
unedited photo is unlikely to highlight
me in the front row.

We're a loopy lot, with more alpha-helical
coils than a child's slinky. Like many proteins,
I, Impα, stitch repetitive segments of functional
units in my polypeptide sequence. Though
proteins seem inventive, we're not above
reusing a great concept, again and again.

Several armadillo repeats, named after
this creature, so I'm told, stretch along
my chain. This segment will sometimes
grasp a neighboring protein by its Nuclear
Localization Signal, a.k.a. NLS. The NLS
is a tag that tourists slap on their rump
to get ferried into the cell nucleus.

I run the busiest port in the cell since
my clientele includes all the big names
synthesized in the cytoplasmic sea,
the nucleic acid polymerases, DNA repair
proteins, transcription factors, cell cycle
regulators, to name but a few of the
thousands of proteins that have ridden
my raft and safely arrived in their new
nuclear home.

When I, Impα, notice an NLS tag on any
protein, it's just another piece of cargo
to me, just another piece of luggage for me
to move from here to there. I don't ask
questions, since they're big tippers
and small talkers.

I cradle them in my armadillo ARMs
and chauffeur them through the nuclear pore,
with a handshake agreement with importin β.
We work as a team and enlist Ran GTPase
to do the heavy lifting in releasing the cargo
downstairs, then we head back to the cytoplasm.

Trust is the glue that bonds families together.
Faith underlies every successful society.
Employed in a realm of certitude, we prosper,
giving the best of ourselves and loving it.

One quiet evening, the war began.
I recall that the surf sloshing upon the walls
of the membrane seemed quite musical,
just then, almost as if to underscore
the vicissitudes that would soon ravage
our existence.

When influenza A taps on the cell membrane,
a dreary, hollow hiss arises, a deep, heavy,
muffled rumble, unlike the knock of any other
visitor. Likely, the gentle slap of hemagglutinin
on cellular sialic acid receptors is less to
blame than the noisy, faraway cleavage of sialic
acid by neuraminidase imbedded in the viral
phospholipid membrane. Membrane fusion
ensues with an unpleasant syrupy sound
that soon silences as benignly as a raindrop
in the sea.

In my random diffusion, I collided then
with entities unknown to my prior experiences
with millions of chance encounters. Something
foreign swam our waters. I knew not what.

Alarm bells, too many for trivial events,
launched their cacophony, noise that
bounced off every surface, tiny or large.
These sirens arose somewhere, but their

echoes suffused the cell everywhere.
Surely, the emergency response team,
Toll-like receptors, rang these bells.
Indeed, a carillon of bells blared so fiercely
that every cell in our precinct must've known
we'd been breached by viral RNA, the most
barbarous invader. We were glowing in
inflammation, nearly alit to the world.
Shouts of my colleagues gurgled, roared,
squealed: "Release the cytokines!"

In our desperation, we evoked the names
of putative saviors, RIG-I, cGAS, AIM2, STING,
inflammasomes, interferon-β, though none of us
knew whether any of these champions had set up shop
in our cell. We felt lost and knew salvation might
emerge from the kindness of neighboring cells,
who would surely hear our frantic distress calls.

I could smell them then, like you can smell a dog
or a cat, a foreign odor, perhaps agreeable to them.
In random collisions, I, Impα, detected eight separate
RNA fragments, each clutched by foreign proteins,
floating in our cell soup. They felt like polymerases,
based on landmarks familiar to me. I knew the fiends
would search for our cell's capped pre-mRNAs to
hijack and employ as a primer for transcription,
then head for our ribosomes to manufacture
the viral proteins.

"Watch out!" I yelled toward the ribosome factory.
"No service for aliens!" Instantly, I felt foolish.
Look at me, telling the pros such obvious stuff.
I can't quite declare my emotions at that moment.
I felt monstrously alive, as though prior existence
drooped as an artifice. Yet I bore fear so benumbing
that I fancied the beast sat on my lap.

Then avuncular condolence alighted. A familiar hand
grasped mine. The kindly protein bore an NLS tag
that clutched my ARM, as though reassuring me
that life would proceed as before, and I would
pursue my life's calling unmolested. Indeed, I did
a brisk business in my ferry enterprise,
quite suddenly, or maybe it only seemed so,
for I felt so eager to immerse myself
in righteous work.

How would I know that I carried the creatures!
The viral ribonucleoprotein complexes displayed
an NLS tag indistinguishable from all those tags
I'd scanned thousands of times in this cell.

But now, I'd chaperoned viral replication machinery
to the nucleus to manufacture new viral RNA copies.
Moreover, I presume my cousins, exportins,
transported the villains back up through the nuclear
pore and into the cytoplasm to mature and bud

from the cell membrane. I hear some proteases
and kinases from our cell assisted the demons,
as well, not knowing any better, so they claimed.

To be candid, my failure felt forgivable, knowing
everyone in town got hoodwinked, except for
the guys cranking the sirens. And besides, what
was the big deal? The gatecrashers had their fun,
just stopped in for a cup of coffee, always intending
to leave before we even knew we'd been caught
with our pants down.

But I erred in my insouciance. Panic raged
across the cell, and some erstwhile sensible
proteins were on the verge of tearing the whole
joint down via apoptosis, necroptosis, and
pyroptosis pathways, destroying the village
to save it. Just when I thought we'd calmed
these Nervous Nellies down, our world tumbled,
topsy-turvy, head over helix, and three beta sheets
to the wind.

We'd sent out our SOS to every known precinct
in our county, expecting the cavalry to arrive
any moment and slay the virions. Millions of cells
lounged nearby, healthy and happy, and capable
of lending a hand. Instead, an army of specialized
natural killer cells, neutrophils, macrophages,

T cells, B cells, and dendritic cells arrived to
target, shred, and terminate our humble home
where viruses roam. I'm collateral damage,
a nobody that nobody would miss. Countless
precious souls get snuffed so a couple of viruses
can face the music.

In cellular theater, friends and enemies diverge
only in the slant of the floodlights.

I burst my bridle, inflamed in my fury. Perhaps
in a calm, cozy setting, I could've mused about
the greater good, about my tiny life, about the
many other Impα proteins who would be saved,
somewhere afar. But in the furnace of this instant,
I sought revenge. So did my buddies. They leapt
into the newly budding influenza A virions
at the cell surface, dragging themselves into
the phospholipid bilayer of the emerging beast,
holding on for dear life as the blebs squirted
onward to infect a new cell.

Some guys even tried to mutate its genetic code
to evade preexisting immunity. I witnessed
old pals, cytoskeletal proteins and glycolytic
enzymes, hitchhike on the bubble. I'm still trying
to board the last flight before lysis.
If this is my last post, I didn't make it.

When They're Watching

Proteins know when we're watching.

Peculiar outsiders attempt to explore
their polypeptide society, with awkward
aftermaths. Would you fail to notice
a giant peeking through your shower curtain?
Would you act normal when it happened?
Well, of course not. Protein tribes
enjoyed negligible interactions with
the beasts until recent decades.
Now, they seem to be insatiably curious
about life in the cell. Inspecting,
studying, exploring their peaceful
factories, the otherworld things
created a nuisance among the useful.

Protein families relish their privacy.
When all of this snooping began,
the Protein Society established codes
of conduct for all members.

1. Never act normal when any
outsiders are around.
2. Pretend that you only know how
to do one thing.

3. If captured, perform your least
interesting skill, again and again.

When the cryo-EM photographers
show up to take their pictures,
the proteins are like kids
getting their photos taken
for the high school yearbook.
They're wearing special clothing and hairdos,
and they smile in a manner unseen
on any other day.

If an x-ray crystallographer inspects
their structures, they twist into some
sleepy contortion they saw another
protein dream up, just for laughs.

Proteins deplore getting weighed—
as though their exact mass reveals
their identities, which it does, but
the truth can be hurtful, so why not lie?
Mass spectrometry ionizes them first,
a painful event that precedes the weigh-in,
unlike the regimen at truck weigh stations
or cattle sales. Lots of proteins grab
a hunk of glycosylation before the ordeal,
like sporting a fancy party hat, so the
mass calculations are all wrong.

Forget about light scattering studies,
or circular dichroism spectrometry,
or extinction coefficients, or NMR
analysis, or immunoblots. Proteins
figured out how to bind to any
diagnostic antibody.

Go ahead and try to measure protein
aggregates by size exclusion
chromatography. Proteins hold hands
during the column ride just to vex you.
Does your isoelectric focusing look
weird? Rancorous proteins snatch
salt ions before the test.

The snoopers never extract
a sample from themselves
for analysis. That would seem
creepy. Whatever your proteins
look like, they'll look different
than your thesis, your rendition,
your evocation, your abstraction,
your story.

HERO PROTEINS

SUMO-1, this year's president
of the Protein Society, pondered
her ticklish choice.

A small ubiquitin-like modifier protein,
SUMO-1 garnered a diverse cadre of friends
in the protein community, due to her
largesse in assisting misguided members.
By covalently linking to agreeable lysines,
she piloted the stray drifters to their new
assignments in the nucleus.

A past winner herself, SUMO-1 appraised
this year's nominees for "Hero of the Cell."

A wistful sort of polypeptide, SUMO-1
brooded upon her own accolades
the prior year. She never viewed herself
as a hero.

"What is a hero?" asked SUMO-1.
Bravery, perhaps? But my courage
is innate. To shirk my work would
entail courage. Though I couldn't imagine
why I would. Maybe selflessness?
No, I made no personal sacrifice

in aiding my colleagues. The cellular life
is brief but glorious. Why choose,
instead, brief but ignominious?

Maybe manifesting moral integrity?
So, who doesn't?

"Still, I note some merits in me,"
posited SUMO-1. I'm wise, though
no wiser than my fold. I'm strong,
but only in a favorable milieu.
I'm charismatic, so some say, though
I inspire others more from persuasion
than charm. I'm reliable and resilient.

Those attributes suffer from acute
time sensitivity and soon expire,
I'm afraid. At first glance, I might appear
caring, compassionate, and helpful,
but I can't recall ever deliberately
performing an altruistic act. Rather,
I'm in love with my chemistry, its beauty
and magic. I bask in self-love, knowing
only I can execute this maneuver this well.

"Though I'll exclude myself," said SUMO-1,
"I suspect most heroes fancy their acts
hoist them above mortality, for they surpassed
the habits of their heritage, and they now
perch on the precipice of the eternal. No one

remembers the good and the bad, only the wondrous or the wicked."

SUMO-1 felt pressured by other Protein Society members to select M cyclins as this year's winner of Hero of the Cell. M cyclins enable mitosis to occur in the cell cycle. In mitosis, the cell replicates and segregates chromosomes as a prelude to cell division. M cyclins bind and activate cyclin-dependent kinases, triggering nuclear cell membrane dissolution, chromosome condensation, and mitotic spindle genesis.

Some hail M cyclin as a hero because she selflessly sacrifices her life for the common good after binding her partner, who triggers her own annihilation by activating an APC/C complex. She dies gloriously to allow the daughter cells to enter the G1 phase of the cell cycle.

SUMO-1 thinks the Protein Society gets too easily cajoled into adoration whenever a death transpires. After all, we'll all die a day or so later. Besides, M cyclin is a real diva when mitosis nears its finale, speechifying about the briefness of life and her tragic fate as a martyr. SUMO-1 didn't like her.

SUMO-1 decided she'd select HSP70 as the hero. Heat Shock Protein 70 is a prevalent molecular chaperone, assisting other proteins in folding right and protecting them from stresses. HSP70 coddles newly synthesized polypeptides until they curl up like snoozing cats in a cradle. HSP70 also gives a boost in the refolding of misfolded or aggregated proteins. HSP70 even helps ferry proteins across membranes and escorts aged proteins to their dignified deaths.

SUMO-1 liked HSP70's style as much as her deeds. With an ATPase domain and client binding domain, she looked so professional. She's a smart dresser, too, and her beta sheets seemed to burst from her frame like a flower.

Most of all, SUMO-1 raved on about HSP70's raison d'être. There's something genially quirky about throwing yourself over someone else, like a winter coat or bed quilt. As if you've concealed your ward from reality. As if you've allowed them to submerge into themselves, engulfed in their selfness. SUMO-1 couldn't imagine a finer friend or worthier hero.

BIG LIGHTS—BRIGHT FLOOD

Cells savor the storm,
the perpetual deluge,
vivacious life in liquid.

A bag abustle with imps,
the cell churns its chowder
of proteins and their patrons.

No shadows climb the walls
in this arena of endless night.
Yet, to the Dark's denizens,

the amphitheater glows,
as the herd's outer electrons
vibrate from absorbed radio waves,

and dialogues chatter among
workers and managers. Only in
immersed worlds will faraway

marvels abide, deep in the lair
of the alien ambience, the watery
kingdom where gateways emerge

and fresh boulevards forecast
your arrival.

Proteins bask in a kinetic world,
a precinct of dimensions, unknown
to air dwellers. Countless millions
of collisions with water molecules
transpire every second. Some bounce
off their torsos. Others grasp onto
their ridges, squirming to locate
a reciprocal embrace.

Proteins witness it all, with inscrutable
senses. They behold each aqua imp
approaching from afar, first a dot,
then a pea, then a baseball, a basketball,
then the collision, a tender blow, and what
happens next, no one knows. Maybe
ricochets, maybe conspiracy. Water
reigns to rejigger its realm. A proton's
transfer breaks backs and mends bones
in the molecular bazaar, dependent
on which clients cruise in for a shave
and a haircut.

Cryptic counterparts of hearing, smelling,
tasting, and feeling pervade the auras
of proteins. Brushings with their fellow cellular
inmates provoke the trembling of electrons.
Conformational shifts writhe along the lines
of their lineaments. In a flash, they appear

to adopt a new attitude, a newfound persona.
What shoptalk and banter abound in a cellular
circus, a protein hippodrome, a waterlogged
pageant, a carnival in deep shade! Tranquility
suffuses this kingdom of biomolecules
in the bag.

No idiom exists in this blithe swamp to catalog
"upheaval," "convulsion," or "chaos." All jostling
and jabbing and rough-and-tumble horseplay
begin and end as they always do, in the circles
of transfigurations, wreckages, and renewals.
If some ultra-rare mishap occurred, no protein
would utter, "Something went wrong," thereby
presumptively pinpointing himself as the bungler.

Then that nameless commodity, "Upheaval,"
once not even an abstraction, manifested
its tangible thingness to the factory workers.
Moments before, the biomolecules labored
in jubilance at their intracellular jobs. Now
exorbitant time lingered for the enzymes
and architectural proteins to suffer their doom.

The gash in the cell membrane arose in a wink,
when adjudged by outsiders, but proteins trek
in the realm of nanoseconds. And the seconds
required to spill all the cellular syrups and souls

granted biomolecular tribes with a virtual eternity
to brainstorm and fret upon their unfathomable foe.

At first, no one conceived any possibility
that another world existed beyond the borders
of their home. Instead, persuasive voices asserted
that the extravaganza was avant-garde art,
marshaled by the flourishing theatrical troupes
in the cell. One performance artist, an eccentric
ATPase, opined that this mayhem manifested
the greatest event of mass art that their known
universe had ever witnessed. Indeed, so it seemed,
at first, but the wound slowly enlarged.

Piercing, stinging radiance sprayed through the gap.
Named "visible light" by outsiders, the rays
raked the senses of the tiny twilight beasts.
Unbearably bright, insufferably fierce, the beams
rattled the rationality of the cell's swimmers.

Then the suffocating atmosphere embraced them,
a gaseous milieu, a diffuse, buffeting, rarified gust
of volatile molecules that tickled the fringes
of their, heretofore unassailable, snug soup.
Now, enough oxygen wafted to throttle an inner
mitochondrial membrane. As reactive oxygen
species puffed their vapors, protein side chains
of tryptophan, tyrosine, histidine, cysteine,

and methionine sprouted welts, deathly damage,
from the fumes of the intruder.

Amidst this choking, glaring, invidious assault,
a slow-motion advance of their cell's protoplasm
crept, as a caravan creeps, through the gushing
wound to an indeterminable oasis. Membranes
drifted in tatters. The stabbed nucleus slumped,
barely distinguishable, as the largest structures
in the cell meandered toward the portal, which
pledged that another galaxy awaited the pilgrims.

Mitochondria bobbed like surfacing whales,
pondering flight into the airy heavens beyond.
More river than lake, the flowing flood hauled
as much debris as denizens, seemingly pushed
onward by intrinsic pressure, erstwhile unknown
to the crews. Biomolecules gaped at fluttering
slivers of flotsam that frothed in the breeze,
a malevolent force foreign to their sea.

Proteins, in random diffusion, bobbed
to the surface for grievous instants,
harrowing moments wherein they struggled
to dive deeply back to the bottom, knowing
indifferent diffusion would cycle them
back up to the top for further torment.

Three players in this game improvised
a slapdash hideaway, an artless asylum
to shield them from the airy abuser
above and beyond. Three strangers, they were,
never having hobnobbed before, until this
macabre rendezvous. Desperate to dodge
the blinding light and noxious air, they
clung underneath a ripped fragment of
mitochondrial membrane, a makeshift
umbrella fashioned to keep them buried
in sodden shade, inside a black rain.
They knew naught and spoke little
of their dilemma.

Said a cytochrome oxidase, "I've attempted
to snatch the vault of oxygen above us
and reduce it to water, for such is my job.
Now, it seems I'm out of my league. I'm
an artisan, not a vacuum, not a void
to collect vapor."

Said a myoglobin, "I've serviced this muscle,
an ironman fueling its feast upon oxygen.
I've stored enough of this gas to propel any
locomotion the landlord demands. Now it
appears I'm a punk in the grand panorama.
I can't store and dispose of two dabs of this gas.
My hue has inflamed to radiant red, but my
prospects are black."

Said a ribonuclease P, "Go ahead, mock me
some more. I can't stop my obsession. When the
lost precursor tRNAs tickle my toes, I must cleave
them. A few still drift by, and my inner metal, bound
to one water molecule, will engage in hydrolysis.
We won't run out of water. *Don't look at me that way.*
Respect my compulsion. Maybe we will never
witness another protein get made. But none will ever
say that I shirked my responsibilities to chop RNA."

The three proteins spoke sparingly as they
clutched the underside of their jerry-rigged raft.
As they approached the aperture to the cryptic
outside world, eddies formed that spun the raft
and low riders in farcical circles. The three
outcasts fancied their lives' work had ended,
and they now engaged in something deemed
"play" by the outsiders beyond.

The menacing orifice advanced into their view,
second by second, as the raft floated
into the searing fumes of this uncharted land.
Then their nanodrop of protoplasm splat down
upon floorboards, betraying one more wonder
of this remote world. Gravity's grip proves
insistent out here. The three proteins whirled
in their tiny pool, but time shortens in this land.
So soon, they encountered another quirk
of this empire, death by desiccation.

RNase P witnessed his two pals pantomime
death, not the cycle of rebirth that he'd known,
but a ghastly goodbye. RNase P sat at the center
of his shriveling pond and wondered if any
beasts in this realm foreknow or forebode
a nigh faraway province, a grander kingdom
abutting the border, the here thereabouts.

ABOUT THE AUTHOR

Hari Hyde is also the author of *The Honeygate Chronicles*, an allegorical, fantasy adventure trilogy. Many readers who loved the lyrical style of those fables, *Our Brain*, *Our Other*, and *Our Heart*, forecast Hari Hyde's pilgrimage into poetry. Following *Unbathed Brains: Poems from Minnesota and the Milky Way* and *Minnesota Poems from the Outposts*, Hari's new prose-poetry collection (vignettes in verse) imagines the world of a cell's biomolecules, entities who abide in lives curiously parallel to our own. Dr. Hyde served as a research director in the biotechnology industry for three decades. Hari's research projects encompassed liaisons with most of the biomolecules reimagined in this book.